Rerouting the Protestant Mainstream

Rerouting the Protestant Mainstream

Sources of Growth & Opportunities for Change

C. Kirk Hadaway &
David A. Roozen

Abingdon Press
Nashville

REROUTING THE PROTESTANT MAINSTREAM:
SOURCES OF GROWTH AND OPPORTUNITIES FOR CHANGE

Library of Congress Cataloging-in-Publication Data

Hadaway, C. Kirk.
    Rerouting the Protestant mainstream : sources of growth and opportunities for change/C. Kirk Hadaway and David A. Roozen.
        p.   cm.
    Includes bibliographical references and index.
    ISBN 0-687-45366-6 (pkb.: alk. paper)
    1. Liberalism (Religion)—Protestant churches—History—20th century.
2. Liberalism (Religion)—United States—History—20th century. 3. Church growth—United States. 4. United States—Church—20th century.
I. Roozen, David A. II. Title.
BR526.H2 1995
280'.4'097309045—dc20   94-32942

Scripture quotations are from the New Revised Standard Version Bible, Copyright 1989 by the Division of Christian Education of the National Council of the Churches of Christ in the USA. Used by permission.

The prayer on page 84 is excerpted from *Guerrillas of Grace: Prayer for the Battle* by Ted Loder. Copyright © 1984 by LuraMedia. Reprinted by permission of LuraMedia, Inc., San Diego, California.

98 99 00 01 02 03 04 05 — 10 9 8 7 6 5 4 3

MANUFACTURED IN THE UNITED STATES OF AMERICA

CONTENTS

CHAPTER SEVEN

NOTES

Suspending Our Suspicions

WHEN A COLLEAGUE HEARD that we were working on a book about church and denominational growth, he groaned, "Oh no." His explanation of why he disliked the subject didn't do much to restore our self-confidence:

"I don't see why we should be concerned about that. Some churches are going to grow and others are going to decline. It all depends on where the Holy Spirit is at work."

Although not an uncommon sentiment in church circles, we nevertheless were taken aback by our friend's suggestion that there was no need for our book (or for our vocation, for that matter).

To make sure we had correctly caught his drift, we continued, "OK, then what is our role as Christians?"

"To do what God would have us do, to be faithful," he answered without hesitation.

"And not worry about whether it results in growth or not?" we interjected.

"That's right!"

A few days later, we asked another colleague why so few mainstream denominational staff people seemed concerned about membership losses. This colleague offered two reasons for the silence. One was a reluctance to admit failure. The second was the perceived importance of all the other things being done by national church leaders. Numerical growth seemed trivial in comparison.

We are not the first, of course, to note that mainstream

church leaders (with a few exceptions) are not very interested in talking about church growth. In fact, interest was greater twenty years ago than it is today. In the mid-1970s large-scale studies of membership trends and church growth were organized in nearly every denomination. Hoge and Roozen's *Understanding Church Growth and Decline* included several of these analyses.[1] In retrospect, this research had many limitations, perhaps the most glaring of which was the lack of integration between social contextual influences and the possibility of institutional response. But the research did help practitioners to frame the issues; and it also helped all of us to better understand the challenges of social change for the church, many of which continue to haunt mainstream churches.

Beginning in the early 1980s, the decision to "turn things around" was made by most mainstream denominations. The United Methodist Church, for example, approved a goal in 1984 to double in membership by 1992; the United Church of Christ voted evangelism a priority from 1989 to 1993.[2] In most cases, the goals resulted in at least some new denominational programs and adjustments to denominational priorities. Yet the decline continued.

Mainstream church leaders grew tired of hearing about membership losses and the ineffectiveness of efforts to "turn things around." The dominant response today is clearly evident: avoidance. We tried to reverse the decline through a renewed emphasis on evangelism. It hasn't worked, and we seem unwilling to take additional steps in that direction, because our theology or ideology won't let us [translation: we're wary of becoming like the evangelical denominations, many of which continue to grow].

So we are left with doing our other important work for God, and we do it the best we can. Indeed, we work hard at it. We are faithful in it. And perhaps, we hope, others will recognize the validity of our work and respond. We hope for a growth response, but such a response does not validate our work. In fact, the lack of response often serves to legitimate our faithfulness. As Milton Coalter, John Mulder, and Louis Weeks note, membership decline is seen by some in the mainstream as "the proud red badge of a prophetic church's courage."[3]

We agree that faithfulness compels one to act on convictions. But we find no integrity in avoidance. Peace, justice, and ecumenical concerns (among those "other important things" that often receive blame for the decline) are certainly important to the gospel. Yet the lack of response by the American population (and, indeed, by persons reared in our churches) should concern us deeply, if for no other reason than that it mitigates our voice of witness on behalf of all God's creation.

The mainstream declines are especially ironic because we live in a society that is more open to church-based religion than just about any other country in the world. The vast majority of Americans hold denominational identities; we see ourselves as spiritual persons; we pray; we hold values that are in line with mainstream Protestantism's theological heritage. And the nation's population continues to grow. It seems that mainstream membership should be keeping up with population growth, at the very least. Yet it is not.

A guiding assumption of this book is that within a theological tradition that affirms God's universal presence among us, one that affirms the partnership of human agency in God's purpose, *membership trends are a rough barometer of church and denominational health.* When churches are growing, things may not all be well, but we must be doing *something* right. And when churches are declining, our actions may not be completely to blame, but we must seriously entertain the possibility that we are part of the problem. In either case, faithful discernment demands that we find out why we are growing or why we are declining. Otherwise, we can be lulled into complacency by growth, or unreflectively absolve ourselves of responsibility for decline.

The purpose of this book is twofold. First, it is to analyze mainstream Protestant church membership trends and the social and cultural forces that influence such trends. Much of this analysis is based on research reported in *Church and Denominational Growth.*[4] We have updated and simplified several charts and graphs from that book, to make the data current and more readily interpretable by pastors and denominational leaders who can make a difference.

A second purpose is to move beyond analytical description to institutional prescription. It is one thing to know why we have been declining; it is quite another thing to know what to do about it. Our prescription, however, is not a cookbook of techniques. More than enough has been written about evangelistic methods and programs. Change is needed at a more fundamental level. For this reason, we risk proposing a general strategy for church revitalization that is not only consistent with our diagnosis of the situation, but also consistent with the theological heritage of mainstream churches. That is, we propose "a new course" for the mainstream that builds on the genuine opportunities for growth latent in our current, theologically liberal, identity.

As is evident by now, this is a book written by Protestants, primarily for the Protestant *mainstream*. As many before us have noted, the term *mainline* is imprecise and difficult to define. In reference to the same segment of American Protestantism, some prefer to speak of *liberal,* or *ecumenical,* or *establishment,* or, perhaps most historically accurate, *old-line.* We prefer *mainstream* because of its emerging popular currency, which makes it a helpful label if properly used in a descriptive, rather than a normative, sense. Descriptively, it identifies a set of Protestant institutions that, as Carroll and Roof note, now share a similar niche in the American religious economy:

> What these institutions share are some common theological understandings about the role of the church in society, memberships with somewhat similar socioeconomic characteristics, a sense of historic religious status, and also increasingly, an awareness that their cultural and religious authority has declined, that as religious bodies they no longer wield the power and influence they once did.[5]

The theological heritage shared by the institutions of mainstream Protestantism is decidedly "liberal"—another imprecise term. By *liberal,* we mean the stream of American Christianity that includes emphasis on: divine immanence; the goodness of human nature and affirmation of individual freedom; an optimistic, postmillennialistic concern for social reform; human agency informed by experientially grounded reason; and interpretive and symbolic, rather than literalistic, approaches to scripture and creed.

More concretely, by *mainstream* Protestantism, we refer to those religious groups which, in the not too distant past, functioned as an unofficial religious and cultural establishment of the United States, and of American Protestantism generally. Among others, the mainstream "members" include: American Baptists, Congregationalists (and other predecessor bodies to the United Church of Christ), Disciples of Christ, Episcopalians, Lutherans, Presbyterians, and the Reformed Church in America.

To speak of *mainstream* Protestantism clearly implies that there are other tributaries within American Protestantism, and as we note in chapter 1, they certainly include what arguably are the most vital and confident groups within American Protestantism today. They therefore deserve our respect, and they do provide important lessons for the mainstream. We also believe that they can profitably learn something from our analysis of membership trends and of the social forces that influence them. But they are not the primary audience for which we write, and indeed, our prescription is intended very specifically for the mainstream.

We begin in chapter 1 by setting the stage—looking at the context in which churches and denominations live, and at their growth or decline in this environment. Much has been written about the shape of American society in recent years. Some authors describe the current situation in militaristic terms, such as culture wars, suggesting that ideological conflict increased as the line between traditionalists and progressives became more sharply defined.[6] Others, especially those speaking from postmodern perspectives, reject such dualisms as a remnant of debunked positivism. They stress, sometimes affirmingly and sometimes disparagingly, the increasing pluralism of Western society and the inherent tension between particularistic and universal identities.[7] Still others nostalgically long for a rekindling of the small-townlike Christian community in the face of the onslaught of secularized individualism.[8]

Contradictory images also characterize descriptions of the American religious scene. Many social theorists continue to describe the current situation in terms of technologically and economically driven secularization. Others promote a "new paradigm" based on selective, niche-oriented growth in an American religious marketplace—growth driven by competition, innovation, and religious "consumerism."[9]

Our goal in the first chapter is to impose some order on these disparate characterizations of American society and its religious orientation, each of which contains at least a kernel of truth. But our overriding concern in this chapter is the perspective that such analyses and interpretations offer on two very concrete questions: Which denominational families are growing? And why are they growing (or why not)?

Having set the stage from a national perspective, in chapter 2, we look at *why* Americans participate (or don't participate) in churches. Here the focus is on individuals and their church connection. What influences whether people *join* churches; what influences whether people *attend* church; and what changes have occurred, over the past quarter century, in the pattern of influences related to church membership and attendance? To understand why churches and denominations grow, it is necessary to understand the actions of individuals. Denominations grow as individuals join churches, and the reasons people join churches are complex.

We look next at congregational growth. The focal question of chapter 3 is: *How* do local churches grow? Research in this area abounds, as does confusion over the most important factors related to growth and decline. We examine the most recent research from numerous broad-based empirical studies of church growth and decline. The more antidotal "wisdom literature" from such church consultants as Lyle Schaller, Kennon Callahan, Herb Miller, and the like is not ignored in this section. However, it is interjected for our purposes when supported by a rigorous body of research. Many things encourage growth, but only a small number are critical. What are they?

Chapter 4 deals with what can be done by declining mainstream congregations that wish to grow. It forms the heart (or more appropriately, given our argument, the soul) of the book. This is not a programmatic, techniques-oriented chapter on evangelism, however. Rather, it focuses on what is necessary for a mainstream congregation to become a vital, spiritually oriented church today. Our research and our experience have convinced us that: (a) growth is a natural by-product of congregational health; and (b) those mainstream congregations that choose to emphasize evangelism (broadly defined) will succeed only if this emphasis is grounded in a more general, institutional vitality.

Denominational growth is our final substantive section. Chapter 5 returns to the discussion begun in chapter 1 on the causes of denominational growth and decline. But whereas chapter 1 focused primarily on demographic and sociocultural factors, chapter 5 focuses on what it is about denominations themselves that fosters (or hinders) growth.

With this as background, and building from the argument for spiritually oriented congregations offered in chapter 4, chapter 6 presents a vision and related strategy for what national mainstream denominational structures can do to become partners with congregations and with emerging social networks, in a growing, vital movement.

We are sociologists who have an abiding appreciation for churches and what they can mean in human lives and in service to all of God's creation. As mainstream Christian laity, we also practice our craft as a vocation. We therefore intend this book as *applied* sociology. That is to say, this book contains not "just the facts." We present and interpret "the facts." But more important, we use them as a base for discerning, prescriptively, where God may be calling us.

It is possible to read this book and learn a great deal about church and denominational growth, but reject our "cure." That's to be expected, and indeed, given the current fragmentation of purpose and thought within mainstream Protestantism, all one can hope for is to be heard without making presumptions about being heeded. Nevertheless, we hope that denominational and congregational leaders will be provoked by what two sociologists have to say about how liberal churches and liberal denominations can grow.

Although we own final responsibility for what we say, and especially for what we suggest, we are deeply appreciative to many for their direct support of our effort. In particular, we would like to thank the Lilly Endowment for its financial support; the twenty contributors to *Church and Denominational Growth* for their gifts of analysis and wisdom; and Paul Franklyn and Thomas Dipko for their thoughtful and caring comments on our draft manuscript.

CHAPTER ONE

Where We Are, and from Whence We Came

IN LATE DECEMBER OR EARLY JANUARY, *Newsweek* devotes most of an issue to the year's best political cartoons, *Time* publishes The Year in Review, and *Esquire* issues its annual "dubious achievement awards." Not to be outdone by these secular magazines, *The Christian Century* and the Religion Newswriters Association compile lists of the year's top *religious* news stories. These lists help to illuminate the current state of religion, churches, and denominations in the United States. Our interest, however, is not in the specific content of the stories, but in the themes that connect them.

Heading up *The Christian Century*'s list of top stories for 1993 was the stream of sex-abuse charges leveled at Catholic priests.[1] To a great extent, the attention given to sex scandals in the church only reflects our national obsession with things sexual and our fascination with the human failings of political and religious leaders—persons who are supposed to live on a higher moral plane than the rest of us. As we consider other "top ten" stories, however—conflicts over homosexuality, abortion rights, euthanasia, cloning of human embryos, and so on, we see that broader issues are involved: ethics, the efficacy of religion, religious pluralism, and even the nature of truth.

Religion is presumed to make a difference in people's lives, but often it doesn't. We expect ministers and priests to conduct lives that are consistent with the ethical values they preach. The occasional moral failing does not surprise us, but we are shocked when ministers engage in behavior that is not only immoral but criminal. Concern is expressed that the scandals will "erode church authority and dissolve the crucial bond of trust between pastor and parishioner."[2] Yet the damage goes beyond the walls of Catholic and Protestant churches. Millions of unchurched and "underchurched" Americans hear about the scandals too, and this only reinforces opinions that most active church members are hypocrites.[3]

Not all religion is seen as ineffectual, however. The top religion story for the Religion Newswriters Association (and the second top story for *The Christian Century*) was the "Apocalypse in Waco," the violent confrontation between David Koresh's Branch Davidian and the United States Bureau of Alcohol, Tobacco and Firearms.[4] The Branch Davidian and other extreme religious sects are apt illustrations that religion *can* affect people's lives and dramatically influence their behavior. Yet many such groups are viewed by the public as examples of "toxic religion."

A religiously pluralistic society must allow religious movements to emerge. This kind of tolerance has its consequences, however, and some of these consequences are disruptive. We learned this anew as human flesh burned in Waco, and it is a lesson with which nation states and religious institutions throughout Central and Eastern Europe are struggling. Religions teach ultimate truth, but how does a society function when it is host to a bewildering array of competing and often dogmatic "truths"?[5] No one can seriously claim a monopoly on truth in this situation, but in fact, many groups do try to assert such claims.

Another top story, for example, describes efforts by the Religious Right to influence society with their version of truth through grassroots actions to control local school board and municipal elections in several American cities.

Still another "top story" was the passage of the Religious Freedom Restoration Act, which reasserted (or reinforced) the First Amendment's free-exercise-of-religion clause. Not surprisingly, it was government action against another "deviant" religious group, the Native American Church, that prompted this legislation. Efforts by the state of Oregon to bar peyote use in religious rituals, and Supreme Court concurrence, are seen as dangerous antireligious precedents.[6]

Religious pluralism leads to conflict *among* religious groups, and *between* religious groups and the state. It is also conducive to conflict *within* religious groups, as factions vie for the ascendancy of their version of the truth. During 1993, several "top stories" dealt with liberal/conservative conflicts over the ordination of homosexuals, the role of women in the church, doctrinal orthodoxy, AIDS education, and the sanctity of human life. Particularly serious at the current time is the controversy in the Evangelical Lutheran Church in America concerning a task-force report on human sexuality. The document apparently "calls for Christians to affirm gay partnerships," according to *The Christian Century.*[7]

With so many groups claiming to hold the truth, and fighting with others that hold different versions of the truth, many Americans naturally conclude that *no one* has the truth, or assume that what is true for you is not necessarily true for me. This has become the "liberal," relativistic alternative to the dogma of evangelical denominations, religious sects, and cults. It is the nondogmatic dogma of the "secular" culture, and it poses a difficult challenge for denominations that want to reclaim inactive church members and evangelize the "unchurched."

Religious relativism is, perhaps, an even more serious problem *within* religious denominations. Religions teach moral values and give answers to ultimate questions, but conflict and confusion over values and beliefs are evident in five out of the top ten religious news stories. Denominational leaders can't seem to decide (or agree on) what is right or what is wrong, what is true and what is false. The result is conflict within their own constituencies and confusion over purpose.

Given these problems, it is not surprising that the final top religion story during the year was the downsizing and restructuring that hit the Presbyterian Church (U.S.A), other mainstream denominations, and the National Council of Churches.[8] Denominations that are at the ever-diminishing center of American culture continued their decline—a slide that began in the mid-1960s.[9] The accumulation of membership losses, coupled with increasing suspicion of denominational hierarchies, inevitably led to a funding crisis at the national and judicatory levels. Staff cuts followed, along with reductions in the functions of denominational agencies.

Increasingly, however, Americans seem to be opting out of these institutional battles over religious truth and political influence. The resulting environment is not particularly friendly for churches and religious denominations, but neither is it particularly hostile. Millions of unchurched and underchurched Americans see the church as a "good thing" for other people and the larger society, but see little value in it for themselves.

This is where we are, and how we happen to be here is the subject of the next section.

Membership Trends: 1950–1991

Membership records from American denominations are not reliable enough to determine the "true" percentage of Americans who are church members. Many denominations do not collect *any* membership statistics, and others report statistics that are grossly inaccurate. Also problematic are the thousands of churches that lack a denominational affiliation of any kind. These difficulties mean that we cannot "add up" all the church members in America, using the *Yearbook of American and Canadian Churches* or other published sources.[10] How many Americans are church members at the close of any given year? No one knows.

Given this lack of knowledge, it was not the aggregate national trend in church membership that called attention to issues of growth and decline. Rather, it was that *some* denominations were growing and others were declining. Mainstream Protestant denominations—Presbyterian, Episcopal, United Church of Christ, Disciples, United Methodist, most Lutherans groups, and some Reformed bodies—each began to decline in the mid-1960s. In most cases, these denominations had never experienced decline, but suddenly began to lose members. Attention to the losses was not surprising.

The fact that conservative denominations continued to grow while mainstream bodies were declining led to obvious research questions: What were those churches doing that mainstream churches were not doing? or What were they doing that the mainstream had *stopped* doing? These were fruitful questions for research in the 1970s and deserve more attention today. We address such questions throughout this book, along with additional questions about the apparent discrepancy between poll data (showing consistently high levels of participation) and roll data (church membership statistics showing stagnation and decline in many denominations). But before we can answer *any* questions, we must look at the trends closely and from several perspectives.

In Figure 1.1, we see trend lines for three denominational "families." Mainstream denominations in this chart include the Unitarian Universalist Association, the Episcopal Church, the Presbyterian Church (U.S.A.), the United Church of Christ, the Christian Church (Disciples of Christ), the Reformed Church in America, The United Methodist Church, the Evangelical Lutheran Church in America, and Church of the Brethren. The total membership of these nine denominations forms the top trend line in Figure 1.1. As we now know all too well, this denominational family was growing rapidly in the 1950s, but saw

FIGURE 1.1

Membership Totals by Denominational Family: 1949–1991

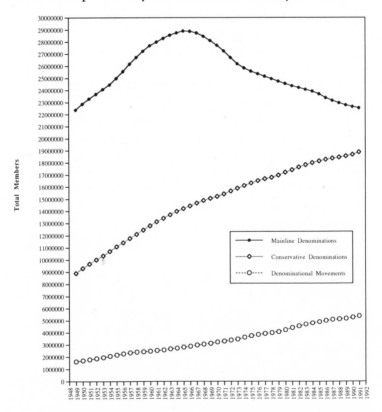

growth turn into decline by the mid-1960s.[11] The decline was most serious in the early 1970s, slowed thereafter, and continues today. The mainstream now has about the same aggregate membership as it had in 1949.

The conservative denominations are highly institutionalized bodies that lack a strong sectlike tension with the larger society. They are goal-oriented *institutions,* rather than aggressive social movements (although most retain some qualities of social movements).[12] We include the following denominations in this category: the Lutheran Church, Missouri Synod; the Southern Baptist Convention; the Baptist General Conference; the Christian Reformed Church; the Evangelical Covenant Church; the North American Baptist General Conference; and the Wisconsin Evangelical Lutheran Synod. Collectively, these denominations gained *more than nine million members* from 1949 through 1991.

We label the third and smallest denominational family as "denominational movements." Most of these groups are smaller Pentecostal/Holiness denominations, aggressively trying to convert the people of America (and the world) to Christ. Other groups in this family differ from Pentecostal/ Holiness churches in theological heritage, but share the same conversionist, otherworldly, movementlike orientation to the larger society. Denominational movements include two Church of God groups (Anderson, Ind. and Cleveland, Tenn.); Assemblies of God; Church of the Nazarene; Seventh Day Adventist Church; Christian and Missionary Alliance; the Evangelical Free Church; the Free Methodist Church; the Pentecostal Holiness Church; the Salvation Army; and the Wesleyan Church. As can be seen in Figure 1.1, these religious bodies *more than tripled* in aggregate membership, growing from 1.8 million members in 1949 to 5.8 million in 1991—a net increase of 4 million members.

Figure 1.1 illustrates the magnitude of net gains and losses for the three denominational families. Conservative denominations have a steeper growth curve than the denominational movements, because conservative denominations added more members. We know, however, that the denominational movements experienced greater *proportional growth* than the conservatives. This is clear in Figure 1.2, where we see total membership each year as a percentage of membership in 1949. When groups reach 150 percent, they are 50 percent larger than their original membership. When they reach 200 percent, they have doubled in membership since 1949. The denominational movements more than tripled, whereas the conservative denominations "only" doubled.

It also is apparent from Figure 1.2 that mainstream denominations were growing at a slower rate than the two other

FIGURE 1.2

Membership of Denominational Families as a Percent of 1949 Membership

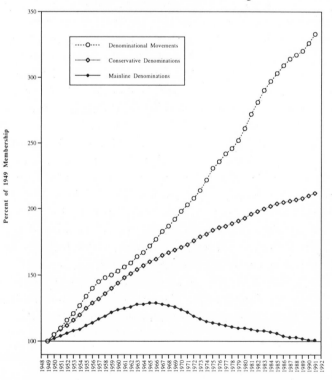

denominational families, even during the 1950s. Further, the growth of the conservative denominational family was only slightly slower than that of the denominational movements throughout most of the 1960s. Later in this decade, however, the growth rates of these two denominational families began to diverge. Growth of the denominational movements continues to outpace that of the conservative denominations.

The two previous figures are helpful to our understanding of denominational trends, but they are easily misinterpreted. For instance, in Figure 1.1, it appears that mainstream growth *suddenly* turns downward in the 1960s. Yet this is not true. In Figure 1.2, it seems that conservative growth was consistently strong throughout the past four decades. This also is not true.

Figure 1.3 provides a more realistic examination of membership change by averaging the *growth rates* of each denomination in its respective denominational family for three-year intervals. These rates are more realistic measures because they plot percentage changes in membership, rather than gains or losses from an aggregate total. In the other charts we can only infer increases or decreases in the growth rate. Here we can see the changes directly. The following points are suggested by Figure 1.3:

- The growth of all Protestant families slowed during the late 1950s.
- The slowdown in growth rates intensified in the 1960s for all Protestant families except the denominational movements.
- The growth rates of mainstream denominations have improved since the early 1970s, but this denominational family is still declining in membership.
- The growth rates of the conservative denominations and the denominational movements are declining, but these families are still growing in membership.

FIGURE 1.3

Average Percent Change in Membership
by Denominational Family

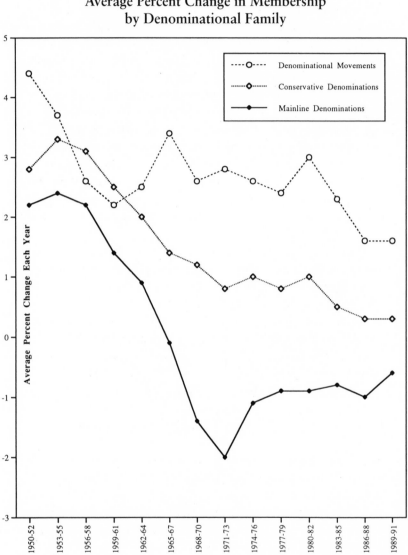

Figure 1.3 reveals that mainstream declines were not sudden. Mainstream growth rates were already dropping in the 1950s. This drop accelerated in the 1960s and finally fell below the zero point (net decline) in the middle of this decade. The downward trend was already established long before 1965, however. Not surprisingly, denominations that were at the center of American culture suffered greatly when the culture became less supportive of traditional institutions. The drop-off in the growth rate was more severe for the mainstream than for the other two denominational families.

Interestingly, the trend line for conservative denominations (the middle line of Figure 1.3) shows a pattern that closely parallels that of the mainstream from 1950 until 1976. The same social and cultural forces clearly affected both denominational families during this period. The pattern for the denominational movements, however, is more volatile and less in line with the general trend of the other two families. The movements exhibited the same downward pattern as the mainstreamers and conservatives in the 1950s, but actually saw growth rates rebound in the late 1960s and early 1970s—the years of greatest cultural upheaval.[13] Denominational movements thrived in an era when traditional religious institutions were under attack.

Finally, since 1980, there has been something of a convergence of average rates of membership change for the three denominational families. Few denominations today are growing or declining rapidly. This may suggest that all institutionalized religious groups—on a continuum from liberal to conservative—are increasingly (and similarly) at risk in American culture.

The end result of this growth and decline is seen in Figure 1.4. American religion has been restructured during the last forty years. The once heavily dominant mainstream denominations are now numerically smaller than the combined membership of the two more conservative denominational families. Even more significant is the fact that the 27 denominations included in Figure 1.4 exhibit an overall pattern of membership plateau since 1967. In a strict sense, the conservative denominations and denominational movements "made up for" the declines of the mainstream. But the United States population grew substantially during this period of plateau. As a consequence, predominantly white Protestant denominations had lost a great deal of "market share" American society since the mid-1960s.

FIGURE 1.4

Cumulative Membership Totals
by Denominational Family: 1949–1991

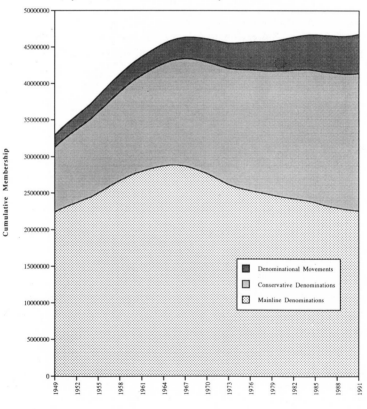

Roman Catholics

The Roman Catholic Church in the United States is growing, according to official statistics, but the more closely we look at their records, the less confidence we have in the accuracy of the reports. More often than not, Roman Catholic membership figures are only estimates of the number of persons in a parish who consider themselves to be Catholic. The sheer number of self-identified Catholics has grown, but poll-based studies show that the average Roman Catholic attends Mass much less often today than was the case in past decades. In addition, disaffiliation is high and switching to other denominational families has increased.[14]

The situation is even worse among Catholic baby boomers.[15] People continue to be born into the Catholic Church, and members continue to see it as THE church. Yet the Catholic subculture is changing. As Penny Marler and David Roozen suggest, Catholics who attend regularly are persons who are institutionally committed and feel that their parish "is warm and meaningful." In other words, they are acting more and more like religious consumers than like a captive audience.

The Catholic Church may be growing, but its rate of growth is probably far below official estimates.[16] Further, much of its growth is due to immigration and high birth rates within certain segments of the Catholic population.

Historical Black Denominations

No portrait of American churches is complete without the historical black denominations. What conclusions can be made about African American churches in America? Unfortunately, no membership trend data exist for this important and sizable family. Nevertheless, it is clear that many black churches are healthy and growing. Indeed, evidence of such institutional health is easily observed by visiting black churches in almost any city at noon or 1:00 P.M. on Sunday. Black churches and Pentecostal/Holiness churches are often packed, with standing room only, in great contrast to the typical mainstream or traditional conservative church.

Are black denominations growing? The apparent health of black churches and the consistently high levels of self-reported church attendance suggest that they are.[17] In addition, Penny Marler and Kirk Hadaway find that black churches in historically white denominations are growing much faster, on average, than white churches.[18] Other sources of growth include the almost "involuntary" nature of church participation among blacks in the rural South and the continued high levels of attendance in the North.[19] The evidence also suggests that cultural changes in the 1960s and 1970s had less effect on black denominations than on white denominations. Birth rates remained high for blacks, and anti-institutionalist attacks did not target the black church. According to Hart and Anne Nelsen, "the black church prospered in the 1960s," even "as conflict over basic values grew."[20]

The only troubling signs for the black church today are the extremely low levels of church participation among youth in the northern inner cities. According to Hart Nelsen and Conrad Kanagy, "the future of the black church in the city is really dependent in the long term on the black church's ability to involve the less educated, younger adults who currently have little predisposition—and possibly even disdain—for it."[21] For the present, however, black churches and historical black denominations appear quite vital, especially those energized by the Pentecostal movement.[22]

Independent Churches

The primary focus of this book is on American denominational religion, and our discussion of membership trends thus far has been limited to that. The American religious scene is broader than denominationalism, of course, and the high visibility of new religious movements during the 1960s, along with the apparent proliferation of independent congregations in more recent years, are helpful reminders of this reality.

Until 1990, national membership figures for independent congregations were nonexistent. Thanks to a cooperative effort between the International MegaChurch Research Center, directed by John Vaughan, and the steering committee for *Churches and Church Membership in the United States: 1990*, we now have data on independent churches for every county in the United States. Unfortunately, however, the available data identifies only those independent churches with memberships of 300 or more, and is most reliable for larger metropolitan counties. So Vaughan's estimate of 2 million adherents of independent churches is clearly an undercount.

The extent of the undercount is unclear. It seems unlikely, however, that the independent church sector would come very close in size to the combined membership of the eleven well-known denominational movements included in Figures 1.1–1.4. We estimate, therefore, that a more realistic count of all independent churches would fall somewhere between 3 and 3.5 million adherents. Further, the movementlike nature of many independent churches suggests a growth curve similar to that of denominational movements. If these assumptions are correct, we can assume that independent churches more than tripled in collective membership during the last forty years.

Disestablishment and Decline

It is futile to attempt to characterize the current American religious scene in simple terms. Some denominations are growing, but others are declining. Churches are dismissed by millions of Americans as either too impotent or too intrusive. There is clear evidence of secularization, yet there also are localized outbreaks of religious revival. Some events indicate a raging "culture war" between religious liberals and conservatives, whereas other conflicts cannot be understood in such polarized terms.[23] These trends and manifestations exist simultaneously in our society and form the cultural milieus in which American churches must operate. Understanding this situation is not a matter of picking a single perspective. It is a matter of integrating diverse, seemingly contradictory, perspectives into a coherent image of reality.

As we see it, the erosion of the cultural center and the disestablishment of mainstream Protestantism provide the keys to understanding "where we are" from a religious perspective. The decreasing power of the mainstream is only a reflection of a general breakdown of the "dominant culture" that was supported and defined by white Protestant Americans. The primary losers in this process were the mainstream denominations which collectively constituted "established" religion for American society. These institutions have much less influence, and the culture has become much more fragmented and secular, no longer serving as a general plausibility structure for a religious people.

The breakup of the religious establishment provided fertile ground for the growth of religious movements, particularly during the 1960s and 1970s. Non-Christian groups expanded enormously in percentage terms, but much larger net gains were recorded by denominational movements which expanded on the far right of the Protestant liberal/conservative continuum. The decreasing power and influence of the mainstream and the increasing size of conservative denominational families led to a much more level religious "playing field." Denominational families must vie for influence on a more equal basis, in an era when their ability to affect societal outcomes is diminished.[24] Not surprisingly, tensions have increased between religious liberals and conservatives.

All American churches and denominations are threatened by an increasingly secular culture, but traditional enemies present easier and more familiar targets. Thus, liberal/conservative "culture wars" persist, despite the fact that the issues of contention seem less consistent with traditional definitions of liberalism or conservatism. The labels *liberal* and *conservative* are losing their meaning, except in symbolic terms. Our conflicts are symptomatic of a loss of power, confirming the impression that American churches are out of touch with the concerns of the millions of Americans who are among us, but not with us.

CHAPTER TWO

Making the Church Choice

IF OUR ONLY PERSPECTIVE OF CHURCH TRENDS in America since the 1950s came from national poll data, we might be perplexed by all the fuss about church growth and denominational decline. According to the Gallup poll, the proportion of Americans who say they are church members today is the same as it was in 1975, and is only a few percentage points lower than poll readings from the early 1950s.[1]

Church attendance rates also exhibit remarkable stability in the polls, particularly for Protestant Americans. According to data from the Gallup Organization, "current self-reports of church attendance among Protestants do not differ significantly from levels recorded in the 1940s, and attendance among Catholics stabilized almost two decades ago after declining in the 1960s and early 1970s."[2]

The stability in church membership and attendance trends among Protestants is clearly visible in Figures 2.1 and 2.2. Church *membership* among self-defined Protestants declined by only two percentage points from 1952 to 1992. Not much of a drop!

The trend line for church *attendance* also is quite flat, exhibiting no consistent up or down pattern since 1939 (see Figure 2.1).[3] Religious commentators frequently cite attendance in 1958 (44 percent of Protestants) to demonstrate just how much

FIGURE 2.1

Protestant Church Membership: 1952–1992

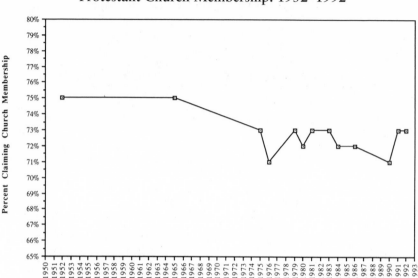

FIGURE 2.2

Protestant Church Attendance: 1939–1991

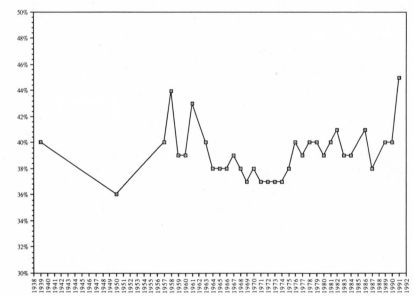

church attendance has fallen in subsequent years. In doing so, they ignore large fluctuations in attendance figures during the 1950s. If we "split the difference" between high years and low years in the 1950s, however, the "decline" in church-attendance rates during the 1960s and 1970s is only two percentage points. And that minor decline was reversed in the late 1970s. *According to public opinion polls, attendance among Protestants is just as high today as it was in the late 1950s.*

If one takes Figures 2.1 and 2.2 seriously, it is easy to conclude that all is fine with American religion, and particularly with American Protestantism. Indeed, various authors have come to just such a conclusion.

Commenting on religious change in a midwestern city, Theodore Caplow and his associates declare:

> The Reverend Rip Van Winkle, Methodist Minister, awakening in Middletown [Muncie, Indiana] after a 60-year sleep, would hardly know he had been away . . . the general level of religious belief and practice is not very different today from what it was a century ago, and the leading tenets of popular theology have remained the same during the past half-century.[4]

In reference to the entire country, Andrew Greeley states: "Whatever may be said in theory about the success of science in its battle with religion, religion does not in general seem to have been notably weakened in the United States during the past half-century."[5]

These conclusions are misleading for three reasons:

- The stable pattern of self-reported church membership and attendance hides serious declines in church participation among younger cohorts.
- The emphasis on membership and attendance ignores an erosion in the overall religious climate.
- The stability of membership and attendance may be an illusion, hiding changes in actual religious behavior.

Boomers, Busters, and Their "Return" to the Church

Conventional wisdom suggests that many young people drop out of church when they move out of their parents' homes, then return to the church when they marry, "settle down," and have children. As with all conventional wisdom, this folk theory is based on a certain amount of fact. Indeed, studies of church dropouts show that most people who leave the church do so in their late teens and early twenties.[6] And many do return. In recent interviews, baby boomer "returnees" reported that some returned to the church "for the sake of their children," or so their children could be "exposed to the church" and its moral teachings.[7]

So what's the problem? The problem is a lack of consistency in the degree to which youth follow this life-cycle church-attendance plan. The plan seems to change from generation to generation, and current generations seem to buy into the first installment, but not the second. Many drop out, but relatively few return.

In the 1950s, the situation was different. Some youths and young adults dropped out of church, but their numbers must have been small, because persons in their twenties attended church at a rate that was similar to that of persons in their thirties, forties, fifties, and sixties. Age or generation did not seem to affect rates of church attendance during that era.

The situation changed drastically in the 1960s, as a unique set of social and cultural changes carried the baby-boom generation with it into young adulthood. Age-specific rates of church attendance and membership began to diverge. From a situation when age differences in religion were minimal, the sixties produced a stratification of religious expression by age. The youngest age cohorts, on average, attended church at lower rates and held weaker religious beliefs. The oldest age cohorts attended at higher rates and held stronger beliefs.

Age stratification has serious consequences for the church,

particularly with regard to membership growth or decline. Young adults and their children are the primary source of new members for religious denominations. The baby-boom generation offered great hope for the church because of its size—if boomers simply behaved the way their parents had behaved a generation earlier. If most remained active in the church; if most had children at the expected rate; and if most dropouts returned to the church, denominational growth would have continued at a rapid pace. But none of these events occurred. Large numbers dropped out, birth rates dropped to record lows, and most of the dropouts did *not* return.

As can be seen in Figure 2.3, the age stratification of church attendance continues. Younger cohorts attend less than older cohorts. Further, the much heralded "second coming of the baby boomers" in the late 1970s and early 1980s did not continue.[8] Attendance rates for older and younger baby boomers leveled off in the mid-1980s and have not increased. Baby boomer church attendance remains well below that of older generations and shows no signs of rising again.

The defection of the baby-boom generation had particularly serious consequences for denominations because of its sheer size and high level of childhood church involvement. Most boomers grew up in the church. They were on membership rolls. Denominational decline was inevitable when many boomers dropped out, unless they were replaced by a large new generation of children. Unfortunately for the churches, the next generation of children did not make up for baby-boomer losses. A surge of growth still would have been possible, however, if the boomers had finally returned to the church and brought their own children. This return was anticipated and hoped for, particularly by mainstream churches, but the return was not large enough to stem the declines in membership.

The attendance rate of each new generation of young adults is critical for denominational membership. It is much more important than a continued high level of atten-

FIGURE 2.3

Birth Cohort Church Attendance Trends: 1972–1990

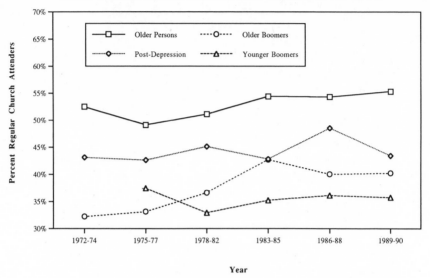

dance among older generations. So unless age-stratified rates of religious participation reconverge at higher (preboomer) levels, membership growth is likely to remain stagnant and below replacement levels.

A Cooler Climate

Church attendance and membership are not the only poll-based indicators of the religious climate in America. Polling agencies also ask about the importance of religion, religious belief, devotionalism, and attitudes toward institutionalized religion. Together, such questions give a much more complete reading of the state of American religion than do church membership and attendance alone. Fortunately, the Princeton Religion Index provides a concise summary of the extensive religious soundings conducted annually by the Gallup Organization. To the extent that a single "best" empirical barometer of the United States religious climate exists, it is the Princeton Religion Index. The index includes questions about: (1) belief in God; (2) religious preference; (3) belief that God can answer today's problems; (4) church membership; (5) confidence in organized religion; (6) feeling that clergy are honest; (7) view of religion as very important in one's life; and (8) church/synagogue attendance.[9] Figure 2.4 shows how index scores and the "religious climate" have changed during the past 53 years.

The graph line seen in Figure 2.4 resembles the decline in mainstream and conservative growth rates (Figure 1.3) much more than it resembles the attendance stability seen in Figure 2.2. It should be noted, however, that the decline in the religious climate did not "bottom out" in the mid-1970s. The decline continued until the late 1980s. Nevertheless, the most dramatic image in the fifty-year trend, and perhaps the most important perspective it adds to our understanding of membership trends, is that the 1960s represented a profoundly transitional decade for religion in America. The tipping point of mainstream Protestantism, from growth to decline in 1965, is only one manifestation of a much broader shift in American religion. Religion began to have less influence on society and on people's lives. It was seen as suspect by some; as irrelevant by others. How then was it possible for levels of membership and attendance to remain so stable? Perhaps it was not.

Just Because I Said I Did . . .

The contradiction between denominational membership trends and poll-based measures of membership and attendance led C. Kirk Hadaway, Penny Long Marler, and Mark Chaves to test the proposition that many Americans over-report their church attendance on national opinion polls. The results should be a "wake-up call" for church leaders. By comparing attendance counts in local churches

to poll-based measures, it was found that "church attendance rates for Protestants and Catholics are approximate-
ly one-half the generally accepted levels."[10] In other words,
attendance for Protestants is closer to 20 percent than 40
percent; for Catholics, attendance is closer to 25 percent
than 50 percent.

FIGURE 2.4

Princeton Religion Index: 1940–1993

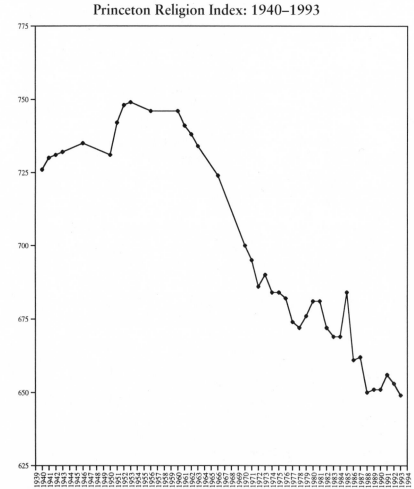

That Americans exaggerate their church attendance is not a big surprise, particularly to church professionals. What is a surprise is the *size* of the apparent gap between what people say they do and their actual behavior.

The study also suggests that the gap has grown.[11] And it is this growing gap that masks declines in actual church attendance. Continued stability in church attendance rates, as reported by public-opinion polls, is an illusion—created by Americans who see themselves as "weekly church-goers," but whose behavior increasingly fails to match their self-perceptions.

So there is no contradiction. Denominational member-ship growth, religious climate index scores, and church attendance rates all declined. The worst years of decline were the 1960s and early 1970s.

Choice, Commitment, and Cultural Change

The erosion in the overall religious climate makes both church and denominational growth more difficult today than it was in the 1950s. Yet some churches and denomi-nations are growing, and millions of Americans attend church each week. In later chapters, we deal with church and denominational growth. Here our emphasis is on the individual: "Why do Americans attend or not attend church?" "How have their patterns of attendance changed?" We address these questions by looking at mainline and evangelical Protestants.

The Mainstream: Habit? or Choice?

Mainstream churches do not expect too much from their members. They are happy when members attend, but they are not surprised or worried when a member skips three or four Sundays in a row. Mainstream ministers understand the complexities of modern life. So when a truant member returns, the minister is unlikely to ask, "Well, where have you been? We sure missed you," or other guilt-inducing expressions of concern.

The vast majority of Americans believe that church attendance has little to do with being a "good Christian." Going to church is helpful and encouraged, but not essential. This view is particularly strong among mainstream Americans and is reinforced by the churches themselves. From the perspective of observer William H. Willimon, "We provided our children with a theological rationale for embracing secularism."[12] Members learn that attendance is optional when anything else comes up—work, summer vacation, out-of-town visitors, lack of sleep, yard chores, bad weather, the associate minister is preaching, the children's choir is singing. The list goes on and on.

So why are mainstream Christians still active in their churches? Some remain active members because they feel that church attendance is necessary. In order to be a good Christian, one must attend and contribute to the church. For many others, church involvement is not necessarily "required," but it is a central part of their lives, providing meaning and helping to "anchor" their self-identities. Church attendance is natural and taken for granted. Fewer and fewer mainstream Protestants fit these profiles, of course, but those who do are likely to be the most loyal members of a congregation.

For most other active mainstream Protestants, attendance is based less on loyalty, necessity, or habit than on *choice*. According to research by Penny Long Marler and David A. Roozen:

> The religious marketplace for liberal Protestants is wide open today. Less motivated by denominational or theological loyalty in the church choice, liberal Protestants attend

church because it is warm, provides personalized meaning, has a clearly "spiritual" focus, is not "too organized," is not "too restrictive," and has just enough but not too much social justice emphasis. Like conservative Protestants, active liberal Protestants demonstrate commitment to the institutional church as an avenue for expressing and cultivating personal religiosity. But unlike conservative Protestants, the influence of church consumerism among liberal Protestants is increasingly unconstrained by traditional religious beliefs and practices or by social background factors.[13]

Mainstream Americans embody a consumer orientation toward religion to a greater extent than do the members of other denominational families. This is not surprising, because the mainstream meanders through the center of a culture where lifestyle choices are increasingly important. As Anthony Giddens notes, "The more tradition loses its hold . . . the more individuals are forced to negotiate lifestyle choices among a diversity of options."[14] Active mainstream Protestants consciously choose to attend church because of the value it provides. Thus, "national membership and attendance trends for liberal Protestants will be largely dependent upon the ability of local congregations to fend for themselves in the absence of strong subcultural norms."[15]

Mainsteam churches should be seen as collections of church loyalists and also of religious consumers. Both groups may share similar levels of commitment to a particular congregation, but the basis of that commitment differs greatly. The loyalist will remain "come hell or high water," but the consumer will seek out a different church if his or her present congregation does not "deliver the goods." These commitments exist, however, in the midst of increasing levels of apathy and marginality among the larger membership of most mainstream churches.

Evangelical Protestants: Circle the Wagons

It is difficult to remain on the margins of an evangelical church by attending only now and then. The only acceptable place to be is firmly inside, an active member. When marginal members show up, they are greeted with guilt-provoking expressions of interest and surprise. Their truancy is noticed. They feel embarrassed and exposed.

In evangelical churches, you have a sense that you are either part of us or not part of us. And if you are part of us, you will participate regularly and believe as we do. Otherwise, you do not quite fit, and you will feel awkward among those like-minded persons. This basis for commitment is taken for granted, because theologically conservative churches attempt to discern and clearly state the "truth"—so that it does not slip away.

According to Harold Bloom, the central feature of what he calls "the American Religion" (typified by Southern Baptists and denominational movements) is this sense of knowing that "I am saved, that I am loved by God, that what I believe is right and ultimate, that it is our responsibility to define truth and morality."[16] Rush Limbaugh, the ultra-conservative talk-show host, asserts that "Morality is a system of virtuous conduct based on the principles of right and wrong . . . . Fundamental right and wrong, such as defined by the Ten Commandments is not arguable, nor should it be."[17] Most evangelical churches know what is right, and they will inform you in no uncertain terms.

Evangelical Protestantism is widespread in this country, but it does not define the *cultural* mainstream. For this reason, evangelical churches must continually distinguish their beliefs and definitions of acceptable behavior from those of "the world." This was less of a problem when boundaries of region and class helped to insulate conservative Christians from the dominant culture. But these social and demographic boundaries have weakened. Evangelical denominations are larger and more powerful today. Income and regional differences are less extreme. Contact and conflict between religious liberals and conservatives have increased. And many evangelical leaders are increasingly critical of peers who attempt to meet human needs by nudging closer to the rhetoric and values of the cultural mainstream.

In this new setting, conservative Protestantism is more protective of its social and symbolic boundaries and, in style, has become even more subcultural. Some leaders, though not all, adopt a "circle the wagons" mentality that drives away persons who do not buy the whole package. As evidence of this change, research shows that "conservative Protestant membership is increasingly characterized by a set of inherited, biblically focused beliefs."[18]

Most evangelical Christians are born into the faith. Socialization efforts are intense and effective. Few drop out or switch denominations, because the conservative church becomes a major part of their social world. Evangelical churches grow by first holding onto their own and, second, through evangelism. Large conservative groups like the Southern Baptist Convention attract relatively few converts, but the emerging denominational movements (e.g., the Calvary Chapels or the Willow Creek Association) and the older denominational movements (e.g., the Assemblies of God and Seventh Day Adventists) attract many. For converts, the decision to participate is not that of a fickle consumer switching from one brand of margarine to another. Commitment, membership, and participation are expected. Indeed, those who switch tend to have higher average levels of participation than those who were reared in the faith.[19]

Evangelical churches create social worlds for their members. They provide webs of relationships and opportunities for participation that tend to insulate the conservative

Christian from competing social groups and the secular culture. Within this environment, distinct social and religious norms allow the individual to maintain his or her conservative church identity in the midst of competing voices. Doing so is not difficult, because one's closest relationships are with like-minded believers.

So rather than eroding conservative religious identity, the condition of modernity has strengthened it by forcing evangelical religious groups to solidify their boundaries, *or* to counterattack by selectively embracing modern technology and method, in service of an alternative worldview. For Americans who hold social values that are at odds with the dominant culture, or for those who are uncomfortable with the moral ambiguities of multiculturalism, the moral and ideological certainty of evangelical churches is quite appealing.

The public "face" of evangelical churches varies widely, of course—depending on the strategy of the group. Some emphasize their distinctiveness from the larger *culture*, whereas others emphasize their difference from the typical American *church*. Both strategies can be effective in the maintenance of group identity, and both messages have appeal to some Americans.

There is clearly some element of cultural accommodation among many evangelical congregations that posture themselves over against "other churches." The Willow Creeks and other boomer-oriented evangelical congregations employ what most would see as secular elements in worship, and remove much of what is traditionally seen as sacred. Yet underneath this seemingly secular public face is a strong evangelical ethos that defies characterization as "relativized." The strategy of "attack" is to draw in the secular "bees" with the familiar "honey" of secular society. But once outsiders become familiar with their new "hive," the strategy changes. Regular visitors are encouraged to become more involved in both the social and the religious aspects of the congregation. In this way, they learn the true ethos of the church and also are drawn into its social world. Some resist the pull, but many do not.

The long-term effect of such a "secular" strategy is unclear—particularly for the maintenance of an evangelical ethos. For now, however, the strategy seems effective for attracting "underchurched" Americans and for generating high levels of commitment.

Negotiating Options and Lifestyle Choices

"A nation of consumers." Perhaps this is an apt description of our nation. It may even be an apt description of the Western world. And it apparently is what former communist countries would like to become. Most people in the world would like to have a choice about a few things. Americans expect choice in all things.

We do not like to be called consumers, however. The word implies conspicuous consumption, using something and throwing it away when something better comes along. *Religious* consumerism is an even more distasteful concept to many clergy and religious leaders. It implies a capricious attitude about something quite serious: one's faith. And yet, Americans are described increasingly in such terms, and their behavior may warrant the characterization. We seek out churches, prayer groups, and Bible studies that give us the most "value" or "benefits," in exchange for the lowest cost. Perhaps that equation is a bit too cynical, because sometimes the personal cost of discipleship is quite high. Still, Americans are much more intentionally free to select or reject a church based on personal tastes. Is it too large, too small, or just right? In the words of a recent classified ad placed in *The Christian Century*, does it have: "skilled preaching and dynamic worship leadership?" How good is the choir; are there enough young people; is it convenient to my home? And in evangelical rhetoric, the consumers can be heard asking, "Will I be fed?" These and a hundred other questions are used by Americans to choose (shop for) a church.

We make a grave mistake if we condemn a consumerist orientation as always lacking seriousness. When we think about it, we realize that our lives are full of serious choices: for a career, a committed relationship, a place to live, and a meaningful way to worship God. The proliferation of choice, and the eclipse of tradition as a constraint for choice, is the modern condition. We live in a world where choices can be overwhelming. Nevertheless, in a world of options, we must choose.

During the emergence of congregations at the beginning of the Christian era, Paul could write to the Romans, "I do not do what I want [follow the Jewish Torah, an obligation that constrains both choice and the emergence of sin], but I do the very thing that I hate" (7:15). Such inner conflicts are not even part of the vocabulary of current religious consumers.

The fading of Christian or other religious tradition as a constraint and guide for choice (or as a substitute for choice) means that individuals are increasingly on their own in developing what we call a lifestyle. We are not completely free of tradition, of course, and norms of "proper behavior" persist (although in greatly relaxed form). Nevertheless, we are free to drop out of the church if we want to, and millions of Americans have done just that. In past generations, they might have remained in the church for the sake of their family, their job, or because the option of dropping out never occurred to them.

We should stress, however, that for many Americans, "dropping out" is not even an accurate phrase. They did not *leave* the church. They merely do not come any longer (or as much). Yet they continue to see themselves as Baptists,

Methodists, Presbyterians—as "churched" people. The things that we say we *are*, and the things that we *do*, do not match very well. As Christians, we say that we value religion for our personal lives, but we find it increasingly difficult to attend a traditional church worship service. Too many other things come up. Too many other things seem more important at the time. Too many other things fit more naturally into our "action strategy" for negotiating modern life—our lifestyle.[20] Many Americans plan to worship each Sunday, and most Americans think they attend more often than they do. They value religion and the church, particularly for what it meant for them in the past. Negotiating lifestyle choices is difficult because modern life is complex. There are more and more choices and fewer and fewer guidelines.

One way to avoid some of the complexity is to adopt the standardized life-planning (from cradle to grave: parenting seminars, diet and discipline classes, reteats, social activities, mission trips, Bible studies, and so on) offered by conservative churches. The choices remain, but most choices are no longer viable options when we choose this life course. We become part of a prefabricated social world, where ideology limits options and defines the shape of acceptable lifestyles. Such an environment seems safe and natural for most persons who are born into it, but for those who are not, joining a conservative church and accepting its beliefs is a major step.

The vast majority of unchurched Americans has slight interest in conservative Christian programming or in restricting their lifestyle choices. The dilemma posed for mainstream church leaders is: How can the church remain a viable lifestyle option for those who value faith but distrust the church? One option is to detach the faith from the church. And that is an option being pursued by millions of Americans today. It should be seen properly as both a source of hope and a cause for concern.

CHAPTER THREE

The Congregation

WHEN RADICAL CHANGE
IS REQUIRED

SOME CHURCHES GROW. OTHERS DO NOT. The list of factors that distinguish growing churches from declining churches is long, because the volume of research, observation, and speculation on church growth is extensive. In fact, several writers of church growth literature suggest that we already *know* enough about church growth. What we need now is for churches to act on the knowledge.

So why don't churches simply add growth-producing characteristics and excise growth-hindering habits? The answer is that many churches try to do so (and fail), and other churches are unwilling to make the effort. The issue, then, is change. Plateaued and declining churches must change in fundamental ways. Simply adding a program designed to help churches grow will not produce sustained growth for a declining church.

In this chapter we look at the characteristics of growing churches, with an eye to change. As we will see, some traits of growing churches are not easily acquired. Location in a growing neighborhood is one such example. Churches cannot import new residents to their community, so population growth cannot be acquired through the efforts of a local congregation, unless their church moves to a new location.

Other characteristics of growing churches *can* be added, through congregational planning and action. Some require radical alterations in the identity, vision, and direction of a church. Others should be viewed as growth-enhancing characteristics—things that enable a growing congregation to grow faster but are not able to turn around a pattern of decline. Plateaued and declining churches cannot grow simply by doing a better job at the things they are already doing. Growing churches, on the other hand, may be able to "fine tune" their programs and ministries and grow even faster than before.

Conceptualizing Characteristics

In *Understanding Church Growth and Decline,* David Roozen and Jackson Carroll suggest that the growth (or decline) of a local congregation is affected by its actions and nature (the institutional), and by its environment or setting (the contextual). They also argue that these factors—the institutional and the contextual—operate at the local *and* at the national levels. It follows that a complete analysis of church growth must consider four sets of influences: the national institutional, the national contextual, the local institutional, and the local contextual.[1]

Social scientists who study church growth and decline underscore the importance of the local context. By contrast, members of the "church growth school," church growth consultants, and other sources of "practice wisdom" emphasize the importance of local institutional factors—what congregations are able to *do* in order to grow. Although practitioners and social scientists generally talk past one another, the issue really is one of balance, rather than neglect.[2] Further, the differences in emphasis between the two groups of experts are highly related to their *different purposes.*

Authors in the church growth tradition are interested in

reaching more people for Christ. Their focus, naturally, is on what churches, as institutions, can do to grow and thereby achieve their evangelistic aims. The context is viewed as either a help in this process or a hindrance, and, while not ignored, its importance is usually minimized. Social scientists often are accused of "environmental determinism" because of their focus on the context. This label is unfair, however, because social scientists never suggest that the local context *determines* whether a church grows or declines. They are interested in finding the major correlates of growth, and thus tend to emphasize the local context for two reasons. First, nearly everyone agrees that the local church *is* affected by its immediate context. And second, the availability (and accuracy) of census data makes it relatively easy to measure the character of the local church setting.

A balanced approach to the debate about context vs. institution gives proper weight to both. It is possible for a church to grow in nearly any context (no matter how "bad"). Examples abound of churches that were able to meet the challenge of an adverse environment and turn it into an advantage. It is also possible for a church to decline in any context (no matter how "good"). Here again, it is easy to find stagnant older churches and "stillborn" new congregations in growing communities. Nevertheless, *the character of the local context makes it that much harder or that much easier for a church to grow.*[3] Institutional actions are sometimes able to "overcome" contextual factors, but churches can never escape the *influence* of their environment.

What about national institutional and national contextual factors? National trends clearly affect religious organizations, but in most cases the influence is either extremely pervasive—affecting all churches in much the same manner—or it is "filtered" through the local context. Thus, the low birth rate (a national contextual factor) is not a major source of decline for a *particular* congregation. It affects *all* churches in a community—to the extent that local residents are part of a national pattern that discourages large families. The impact of national contextual factors on local congregations is seen primarily at the aggregate (denominational or societal) level. If most congregations are growing, then the national *context* for growth is probably "good."

The influence of denominational ethos and actions on local congregations is similarly difficult to identify. Differing denominational growth rates suggest that national institutional factors have a definite effect on church growth. Such differences can be seen even at the local community level. So, for instance, if the Lutheran churches in an area tend to experience more growth than the United Methodist churches, the difference may be attributed to national institutional factors (all other factors being equal). This does not help explain why some Lutheran churches grow faster than others, but it may help to explain the growth of Lutheran churches as a group.

Predisposing Factors

As we have noted, certain characteristics predispose congregations to growth (or decline) and are difficult or impossible to change. Most of these characteristics are contextual in nature, but other characteristics—age of the congregation, size, and denominational tradition—also can be considered "givens" for a local church.

Demographic Influences

Population growth, particularly as evidenced by new housing construction, remains a major source of church growth today. Churches in growing areas grow faster, on

average, than churches located in areas of population stagnation and decline. This is true for all churches—white,
African American, or ethnic. Predominantly white churches grow best in areas where the white population is growing, and black churches grow best in areas where the
African American population is growing. This is hardly a
surprise. Most clergy know from experience that churches
in growing suburbs are more likely to grow than are
churches in declining inner-city neighborhoods.

Apparently, however, the impact of the demographic
environment on churches in the United States diminished
in the last decade. Ironically, with so much notice made of
change all around us, the reason for less impact is less
change. Fewer churches are surrounded by booming suburban neighborhoods, and fewer churches experience
rapid racial transition in their communities. The growth of
"programmatically poor" churches in suburban neighborhoods is less likely—as is the decline of "programmatically
rich" churches in racially changing communities.

The slowdown in demographic change has had both positive and negative effects on church growth in America.
Fewer churches find themselves in crisis resulting from
"white flight," and as a result, fewer churches are closing,
merging, or moving. The bad news is that it is more difficult
to start new suburban churches today. Suburban growth is
less explosive and of a different character than before.
Growth is "spotty" as developers purchase large tracts of
land, often far removed from one another. Additionally,
leaving room for church sites in these planned developments
is less of a consideration than it was years ago.

The Impact of Age

Older churches and churches dominated by older persons are less likely to grow than are newer churches and

those with a large proportion of younger adults. The presence of school-aged children also is associated with church growth.

Newer churches tend to grow faster than older churches. This is a consistent finding in research across denominations.[4] But it is not so much that old age hurts; it is that being younger helps. New churches have a "window of opportunity" for growth. After about fifteen years, however, the likelihood for growth drops. To a certain extent, the growth of young churches reflects their location. Many are in growing suburbs.[5] But even when we control for population growth, the influence of (young) age remains. As Daniel Olson suggests, newer churches assimilate newcomers more easily than older churches because the cliques and other close-knit groups that prevent many newcomers from joining the community life of older congregations do not exist.[6] Furthermore, new congregations tend to have more focus and direction than older congregations. They are trying to create "a new thing" and are mobilized for action. The enthusiasm and excitement of a new church is contagious.

Younger church members also help churches grow. Churches that are dominated by young families tap into the largest population cohort—baby boomers and their children. Of course, some of this success is a result of sheer demographics. Churches located in growing suburbs have a "ready supply" of younger families, whereas churches in older neighborhoods have proportionately few available. Demographics are not the whole story, however. Younger adults are a hard-to-reach population. Churches that are able to reach this group are doing something beyond "business as usual." They are offering programs and activities that no one else is offering, *or* they are offering a superior package of "products." Baby boomers, after all, are church shoppers who make the "church choice" only after careful deliberation.

Congregations dominated by older members present a number of growth barriers. These churches tend to be located in older residential neighborhoods. Their programs and worship styles may not fit the needs and interests of young families and single adults. And as these churches age, the situation often becomes worse. Members die or move away, and they are not replaced. The concentration of older persons increases and the church becomes even *less* likely to attract young adults. For many reasons, then, churches with disproportionate numbers of older members are less attractive to younger prospects.

Denominational Tradition

As discrete subcultures, denominational families either encourage or discourage growth. The liberal mainstream subculture, for instance, is not particularly friendly to growing congregations. Even when researchers control for evangelism, commitment of members, location, and other factors, the churches in conservative, evangelical denominations fare better than the churches in mainstream denominations.

In mainstream denominations, growing churches and their leaders are often considered "suspect." The pastor of a large, growing United Church of Christ congregation in Connecticut even suggested that other mainstream pastors think his church must have "sold out" in order to grow— resorting to questionable marketing techniques and other "gimmicks." Growth itself is not considered a bad thing by mainstream ministers, but rapid growth is such a rarity that it often is assumed that a growing mainstream church is nothing more than a "conservative clone congregation"—an evangelical church with a nominal mainstream affiliation. This view is so pervasive that some mainstream pastors are embarrassed to have books by certain growth-oriented authors on their bookshelves.

It is also true that a sizable proportion of church members in mainstream denominations don't care whether their churches grow or not. It is not that they are explicitly antigrowth, but they are uncomfortable with evangelism and they like their church the way it is. Growth takes effort and necessarily brings change. New members are a threat to the familylike feeling of a congregation. So without an ethos of evangelism, mainstream members are unlikely to work to bring in newcomers. Under these circumstances, is it any wonder that growth rates are low in mainstream denominations, regardless of the other good things their churches might be doing?

In many other denominations, an ethos exists that encourages growth-related activities and insulates the denomination from societal changes. This is particularly true of denominations that retain the missional character of movements. The nation and its population are seen to be in need of change. People must be converted in order to save them from eternal damnation. This ideology is a powerful motivation for evangelism, and for those who believe, church growth is a visible sign of success in reaching the world for Christ.

But growth is not the primary goal for conversionist movements.[7] Rather, growth is the natural consequence of living out the ideology. Growth-related efforts will continue, regardless of their immediate success. For this reason, evangelical churches are less affected by their social contexts than are the more institutionalized mainstream churches. Aggregate rates of growth for evangelicals may parallel the trends seen in mainstream denominations, but evangelical churches tend to fare better in both "good" times and "bad."

Finally, public perception of a denomination is important to the growth of its churches. This is apparent in the recent growth of the Episcopal Church and the Unitarian

Universalist Association. These denominations began to grow a few years ago while the rest of the Protestant mainstream continued to decline. But they did not work any harder at growing than the other mainstream denominations. Instead, it would seem that one key to their recent growth was the *perception* of distinctiveness. Unitarian churches are seen as extremely liberal and open-minded. Whether one's religious perspective is liberal Christian, Deist, pagan, or agnostic, all who are interested in the spiritual search are welcome and appreciated. Unitarian churches give personal and social legitimacy to persons exploring religion in nontraditional ways. The Episcopal Church is equally distinctive, at least in terms of its public perception. It is often seen as an open-minded, liturgically oriented church for high status (or status-conscious) Americans.

Variation by Location and Church Type

Factors that predispose congregations to growth or decline affect churches indirectly as well as directly. For instance, we find that smaller churches and churches in rural areas are less influenced by their environments *and* by efforts at institutional change.

In rural areas and small towns, rapid growth is difficult. Rapid decline also is very unlikely. This tendency toward stability, rather than growth or decline, results in part from demographic factors. Rural areas and small towns experience less dramatic change in population than more metropolitan neighborhoods. There is no suburbanization, no urban decay, no white flight, no racial transition, no rapid population growth, and no rapid population decline in most rural areas. But institutional factors also are at work there. Rural churches and small-town churches are slow to change. These typically small congregations often are dominated by longtime members who prefer for things to be done "like they've always been done." For contextual and institutional reasons, therefore, not much seems to affect the growth of churches in small towns and rural areas. And pastors who climb the rungs of the denominational ladder by starting in small-town churches are soon conditioned to expect that little *can* be changed.

For churches in metropolitan areas, the situation is entirely different. Great demographic possibilities exist for growth and decline. Furthermore, urban churches appear to be more open to change than rural churches. It follows that it is easier for urban pastors and lay leaders to institute a process of revitalization.

Church growth also is more likely in certain parts of the nation—particularly in the South—than it is elsewhere. In general, the subculture and demographics of the "sunbelt" support churches. Some declining mainstream denominations are growing only in the South. As shown in a study by Wayne Thompson, Jackson Carroll, and Dean Hoge, correlates of growth are stronger in the South than in the North.[8] Programmatic growth strategies work best in this region. Regional factors, then, tend to encourage (or discourage) growth.

What Can Be Done About Factors That Can't Be Changed?

Do not use the context or the age structure of your church as an excuse for membership decline. Nor should you blame your denomination. The purpose of this discussion is not to let declining mainstream churches "off the hook." Rather, our purpose is to provide a "reality check" for any church that wishes to change. Who you are as a church, as well as where you are located, affects what you can become.

Radical Change Required

Programmatic efforts to achieve growth often result in more activity than sustained growth. This "activity effect" is seen clearly in program-evaluation studies by C. Kirk Hadaway and Marjorie Royle.[9] Growth consultations and programmed growth campaigns often produce a flurry of activity in a congregation. This activity may produce growth in the short term, if the level of excitement in the congregation rises and is channeled into activities designed to attract and incorporate visitors. But that kind of growth rarely lasts very long.

This finding is a little distressing, because one of the major reasons for studying growth and decline is to determine what changes must be made in order to transform nongrowing churches into growing churches. Clearly, doing so is a difficult process. Why? Because in order to grow substantially and to continue to grow, lasting changes must be made in the identity, vision, and direction of nongrowing churches. This attitudinal shift is akin to heart patients changing their diet and lifestyle. Cutting back a little here or there won't do the job. Radical change is required in order to restore the patient to health!

As mentioned earlier, church growth writers contend that we now know what churches must do programmatically in order to grow. The problem is to persuade churches to do what they ought to do. This is a tall order, because actions flow from identity; actions cannot simply be applied like a thin veneer to the surface of a church. The change must be deeper.

Most growing congregations are not ideal examples of a New Testament church, regardless of the claims of experts and church leaders. Rather, most are growing because they are relatively young, open, and accepting institutions, with a clear purpose and direction. They know who they are, and they want others to share their excitement. They also are located in growing communities or among receptive populations. Plateaued and declining churches, by and large, have lost their youth, direction, open orientation, and growing environment. If they are to grow again, they cannot reclaim their youth nor their environment. So they must work on their identity and direction. They must become purposeful, open communities of faith. They must become *churches,* rather than growing voluntary organizations.

Commitment and Desire for Growth

The members of growing churches are more active, on average, than the members of nongrowing churches. Commitment and interest levels are higher. Growing churches "feel" different from nongrowing churches—and this climate difference is both a *result* and a *cause* of growth. In growing churches, there is a sense that this is "the place to be." Members don't want to miss out if they are in town, so they attend more regularly.

Desire for growth also is related to increased membership. Desire for growth leads to institutional actions designed to produce growth. The fact that members want to grow also helps churches in other ways. All churches say that they are friendly, but growing churches seem friendlier and more welcoming to *visitors.* Churches that desire growth exude a different "spirit" that visitors find attractive. Members want to share what they have with others, and visitors know it.

Commitment and desire for growth are closely related. Growing churches have something to which people can be committed and about which they can be excited. This is more than a set of desirable activities or programs. *There is a strong sense of purpose that flows from a distinct identity and vision.* The church has a mission and lives are being changed. What the church is and what the church is doing create a compelling sense of value. Members tell others about it, whether or not they are told to do so or are trained in personal witnessing techniques. Again, members want to share what they have with others. Having more people in the church is a tangible sign that the "good news" is being spread.

Evangelism and Outreach

Evangelistic outreach is a church's single most important growth-related action. Even though some authors have downplayed the effects of evangelism in reaching the unchurched, or have asserted that evangelism and church growth should be separated, the empirical evidence suggests that outreach *is* extremely important to church growth.[10]

We cannot overemphasize the importance of outreach, evangelism, recruitment, or whatever term is used to describe efforts to welcome new people into the life of the church. Indeed, when statistical controls are in effect, evangelistic activity is the one program variable that retains a strong relationship to growth. High quality worship, Christian education, and many other programmatic variables are related to church growth, but most have little independent effect. By contrast, the independent effect of evangelistic activity is undeniably strong.

We use a broader definition of evangelism than that which refers to door-to-door witnessing or street-corner preaching. As Daniel Olson puts it, the key is "outward orientation." Churches that are primarily concerned with their existing members' needs are unlikely to grow.[11]

The importance of evangelism and outreach naturally leads church practitioners to prescribe more of it for their patients. As noted earlier, however, this rarely works. If members were excited about their church (or their faith) they would be telling other people about it anyway. Evangelism, then, flows out of a sense of purpose, excitement, and mission. And this "sense" must exist before evangelism makes any sense. Under most circumstances, an evangelistic program is useful only to channel a preexisting interest in outreach.

In a few situations, however, it is possible for an evangelistic program to trigger the revitalization of a congregation. The church becomes truly "evangelistic" once it is revitalized (not before), so it is important to separate the cause and effect. The program helps the church in the process of revitalization, but it does not transform the church into an evangelistic congregation. In situations where this occurs, the pastor and a few lay allies begin to tell others in the community about their faith and their church. If these efforts are accompanied by a sense of excitement and expectancy in the worship experience, people will be attracted, and lives may be changed. In a way, the pastor and lay leaders begin to model a new or renewed vision for the church. If the vision is compelling, others will be attracted to it. The result is revitalization.

The reader should remember that any action naturally produces a reaction. Resistance to radical change will be great. An emphasis on evangelism means that other valued things receive less attention. And as noted earlier, new members bring new relationships and the breakdown of "the way it's always been done." Change is risky, even when it is successful. This is one reason many pastors avoid the role of the "change agent." They want to keep their jobs.

The Impact of Ideology

Earlier studies of United Presbyterian and Southern Baptist congregations found a modest relationship between theological conservatism and church growth.[12] Current research offers a more complex perspective. Conservatism remains a minor correlate of growth among Southern Baptist churches, but in Presbyterian churches, there is now a small association between church growth and theological *liberalism.*[13]

A connection between theological conservatism and growth is implied in the work of Dean Kelley (*Why Conservative Churches Are Growing*). Kelley's major point, of course, has nothing to do with conservatism or growth *per se.* His primary thesis is that "strict churches are strong."[14] Conservative churches tend to be strict; strict churches tend to be strong (in terms of commitment and purpose); and strong churches tend to be growing. The connection is not direct, but it follows logically that conservative churches should be growing. They are, or at least they were, but the reasons for this growth seem to have little to do with being strict. Even though conservatism is related to the growth of some denominations, measures of strictness are not correlated with congregational growth.

Due to lack of empirical support and limited usefulness for understanding local congregations, social scientific research into the "Kelley thesis" dried up nearly a decade ago. In recent years, however, the debate has been re-energized through the work of Laurence Iannaconne, Roger Finke, and Rodney Stark—particularly since the 1992 publication of Finke and Stark's *The Churching of America.*[15] We will have more to say about this approach in the section on denominational growth. At this point, we will only suggest that the key issue for churches seems to be a compelling *religious* character (in terms of ideology and *experience*), not whether the content of that character is liberal or conservative.

Removing Barriers and Tweaking the System

There are many things a church can do that will enable it to "do a better job." We divide these actions into two groups: removing barriers and "tweaking" the system. Removing barriers refers to efforts to minimize or eradicate characteristics that are detrimental to the growth of a congregation. Tweaking the system refers to minor improvements that enable healthy organizations to "fine tune" their successful programs and strategies. Tweaking efforts will not result in the kind of organizational transformation needed to revitalize a declining church, of course. But they can help an already vital church achieve its full potential.

Removing Barriers to Growth

Churches must have facilities that allow for growth. Constructing or renting larger facilities may be the answer, but multiple worship services should precede any effort to build a larger worship space. A certain level of crowding is good. A crowd gives the impression that "something is happening." Yet the 80 percent of capacity attendance rule seems to work. When a church reaches this point, future growth in worship attendance is unlikely.

Visitors should feel welcome. It follows that churches should stop doing many things that confuse visitors and make them feel like outsiders. Unchurched visitors are unlikely to know what a narthex is, much less where to find it. Similarly, churches should stop assuming that visitors will know how to find the Sunday school, the fellowship hall, or where the "coffee hour" is to be held. The issue is not merely friendliness and hospitality; it is an appreciation of the visitors' perspective.

Churches should continue church programs during the summer. Essentially shutting down during the summer gives the impression that church attendance is unimportant and leads to a habit of skipping church. It also discourages families from attending, since child care may not be provided during the summer months.

Churches should not schedule church school during the worship hour. Doing so means that adults never experience Christian education and may never participate in small groups. It also means that children rarely experience worship. Is it any wonder that children drop out when they "graduate" from church school? They have no experience in worship, so why should they attend? Our one-stop, "filling station" churches are undermining the faith development of both adults and children.

Ineffective pastoral leadership is another major barrier to growth. The pastor must take the lead in establishing and living the vision of the church. Too often, the pastor takes the lead in *killing* the vision by minimizing its importance. Involvement in outreach is also critical, because it demonstrates excitement about the church and its vision.

Finally, the failure to follow up on visitors is a major barrier to growth. Some effort must be made to contact visitors shortly after they visit a congregation, even by churches that are doing everything else right. A personal contact is best. A letter is better than nothing.

Tweaking the System

Churches that want to move beyond the basics of outreach (contacting visitors and informal invitations to friends) should consider an organized outreach program. It should be remembered, however, that doing so only makes sense for churches that are already "vital." If members do not have any good news to share about their faith or their church, organized outreach will fail.

Supplying name tags for everyone (not just for visitors) is another effective growth-related strategy. It makes newcomers feel welcome. Members are able to greet visitors by name, and visitors can learn the names of members without the pressure of asking people to repeat their names.

"Visitor Sundays" also help churches grow. Again, they help only if there is something exciting to invite visitors to experience, and if the church is interested in assimilating the visitors who are attracted. The church must be a vital organism with identity, vision, and direction. Churches with such vitality are able to use Visitor Sundays to create a surge of excitement and generate lists of membership prospects. Unlike other types of voluntary organizations, growing churches want as many "free riders" as they can get. Persons who participate but do not yet contribute are the pool from which committed members are drawn.

Growing churches encourage the formation of new groups and new ministries. Kennon Callahan's emphasis on a few programs that are well done is important in terms of developing the identity of a church.[16] For a growing church, however, the emphasis should shift to multiple ministries. If there is a need, the church should try to fill it using lay leadership whenever possible. This empowers lay leaders, helps create new lay leaders, increases the "value" of church membership, and provides new "avenues of entry" for potential new members.

Many other growth-related activities could be added to this list.[17] All institutions can be improved, and the means for improvement are varied. Still, the key point is that directionless organizations cannot begin to grow by doing a better job at what they are currently doing. They must be transformed in terms of identity, vision, and direction before they can begin to "tweak the system." In the next chapter, we explain the basis of this transformation for mainstream congregations.

CHAPTER FOUR

Mainstream Church Growth

MARTIN MARTY DESCRIBES A 465-member Lutheran congregation in Nebraska. It is, he says, "one of those presumably irrelevant, redundant parishes that the church growth experts say should be left to die or be bulldozed to make room for a megachurch."[1] Yet that church just celebrated its centennial last year by raising and giving away $100,000 for missions. Marty tells its story as "counterevidence" to the perception that mainstream churches are lacking in creative leadership, interest in missions, and even the Spirit of God.

Martin Marty's story should concern church leaders for several reasons. First, it reveals the widespread perception that only independent, laid-back, celebrative, evangelical megachurches provide viable models for growing churches in modern-day America. Second, it reveals the widespread perception that mainstream churches are sad, self-absorbed institutions, irrelevant to the future of American Protestantism. These perceptions are clearly *mis*perceptions that Marty helps to identify. Nevertheless, implicit in the comment, we also find the tendency of mainstream church leaders to ignore serious problems in our churches. No one wants to "bulldoze" these churches, but their deficiencies are quite real and deserve serious attention.

In this chapter, we argue that the problems inherent in mainstream Protestantism cannot be ignored. Any cure for the decline must confront these issues head-on. We also argue that a solution is most likely to be found among vital *mainstream* congregations, rather than among growing evangelical churches.

The Nature of the Beast

Many people still attend church regularly, and, as noted in the previous chapter, Americans are acting more and more like religious consumers. Indeed, questions about quality, warmth, and "getting something out of church" are more important now than in the past. Nevertheless, even active churchgoers (not to mention church dropouts) frequently describe worship services in their churches as "boring," and other church members as "not very friendly." In fact, according to recent research, Martin Marty's Lutherans are particularly unlikely to describe their congregations as "warm," or to say that their "congregation helps members become more loving and compassionate."[2]

Motivations for continued church involvement are varied. Many Americans still attend church because they think they *must* attend. Others are tied to their church through a web of social relationships. Still others extract personal religious meaning out of worship, in spite of the best efforts of their church to trivialize the experience. Some people attend church for motives other than religious meaning or personal fulfillment—*but not as many as in the past.*

More and more American adults—even those who consider themselves to be "religious"—simply feel no compelling reason to attend church. They don't feel guilty about being absent, they are disconnected from church-related social networks, and they didn't get much out of it the last time they were there. For example, after a somber and penitent Palm Sunday service at a well-known church, a woman called the pastor and remarked,

"I go to church only two Sundays a year—Palm Sunday and Easter. I expect it to be a pleasant experience." American adults also have many other options available for social interaction and spiritual development. So even if we ignore demographic influences (such as low birth rates among middle-class white Americans, the primary constituency of the mainstream) and indifference to evangelism, mainstream church growth still would be problematic.

The most fundamental problem for the ebbing mainstream is the lack of compelling reasons for people to participate. It is no secret that many mainstream churches, and all mainstream denominations, have lost confidence in who they are and why they are. Mainstream church leaders readily admit to an institutional identity crisis. In efforts to establish a new direction, they frequently voice lofty-sounding ideals. They proclaim that we are an inclusive church; we are a church on a mission; we are a welcoming church . . . . But in reality, mainstream churches are drifting, and they are drifting within an *un*reality. It is an *un*reality because mainstream churches, by and large, continue to cling to an establishment model of being THE church, when in fact they no longer have the captive culture or subculture for such a model to work.

Mainstream churches, for the most part, want to hold their services, perform their rituals, minister to the sick and needy, provide warm community attachments for their members, and be at the center of civic life. That is, they want to be parish churches for homogeneous communities which presumably accept their necessity. Nothing is wrong with this model in the abstract. Indeed, it worked well in another era. But diversity has fragmented that by-gone homogeneity, and few people presume the necessity of church membership.

Mainstream churches tend to assume that they *naturally* provide religious meaning. And in the false security of this establishment presumption, they no longer give careful and primary attention to this most critical (and problematic) function of church life. How ironic that even Roman Catholic churches, with their long history of being THE church, don't make this mistake. People expect churches to be *religious* institutions, not social-service organizations or social clubs. According to Leonard Sweet, "Nobody talks about God, or at times is even allowed to," in mainstream churches. "The jargon of liberal theological discourse . . . is drawn from the worlds of psychology and business. The dominant passwords of the church today—caring, sharing, inclusive, intentional—symbolize the lack of identity and uncertainty of address that characterize the liberal theological mind."[3]

Mainstream churches have appropriated the "don't ask, don't tell" approach to God that guides public discourse. Stephen L. Carter argues, in *The Culture of Disbelief,* that to most Americans, religion is "something that should be believed in privacy, not something that should be paraded; and if religion is paraded . . . it likely will be dismissed."[4] Persons who parade their religious beliefs in public are seen as intolerant, religious fanatics who are trying to impose their religious and moral beliefs on others. The result, according to Carter, is a "flight from religious dialogue" that restricts the ability of religion to be a moral force in society (through religious institutions or through individuals acting on their personal religious beliefs). To this, we would add that the "flight from religious dialogue" also restricts the ability of religious institutions to provide religious meaning for their members.

The fear of intolerance and imposition is so great that Americans rarely talk to one another about religious issues, beliefs, and questions. This fear extends to discourse in mainstream churches. In fact, it is likely that open, tolerant, mainstream religious denominations helped to *create* the pervasive fear of religious discourse that Carter observes in American society. The values of religious tolerance and theological openness are paramount within the mainstream. Greater effort is made to communicate our acceptance of diverse views than to communicate what we do, in fact, believe about God.[5]

People are searching for spiritual connection and religious meaning. They want "to have their lives make sense," to find answers to ultimate questions, and to experience something beyond themselves—"wholly other" or "holy other."[6] Nearly everyone in American society believes in God, even many of those who do not express a deep longing for such a belief.[7] People *expect* churches to provide a setting for religious experience and answers to ultimate questions. Instead, mainstream churches seem to fear religious experience and avoid "imposing" answers. "Liberal Protestantism has not given its members eyes in the night," despite the fact that most Americans say they are interested in "spiritual things."[8]

Mainstream churches deaden religious experience among their members because they give it no visible expression. They relativize it; they rationalize it; they bury it in rote tradition. Ironically, their openness to other religious understandings gives mainstream "seekers" permission to explore their spirituality elsewhere, on their own—without any assistance, guidance, or support from their church or from the rich tradition of Christian spirituality and mysticism. As a result, interest in spiritual formation has led spiritually oriented mainstreamers away from the church, most frequently into individualized expressions of religious experience, but also into evangelicalism.

Evangelicalism Is Not Enough

Obviously there is a problem. Is there a solution? We think there is, but it is not found in the direction in which most church growth consultants would have the mainstream look—namely, to conservative Christianity or popular evangelicalism. The mainstream as a whole (or as whole denominations) will fail in an attempt to adapt such models for their own use. Our advice is based on more than just a personal bias toward the Schleiermachian roots of the mainstream's liberal theological heritage. Several pragmatic reasons support this conclusion.

First, few mainstream congregations can be transformed into the narrowly doctrinal and prescriptive institutions of conservative Protestantism. We have no doubt that strong doctrinal and prescriptive boundaries can be effective sources of commitment for some people and in some congregations. But for the mainstream, such a strategy of renewal would, in most instances, alienate existing members and preclude any hope of reaching the mainstream's unchurched constituency—most of whom reject doctrinal and narrowly prescriptive approaches to religion. Clearly, there must be a solid grounding to mainstream Christian faith, but neither the mainstream's theological heritage nor its comfortably middle-class constituency will tolerate narrowly defined creeds for personal conduct and belief.

Second, the vast majority of mainstream congregations will resist imitating what might be called popular evangelicalism—that is, the marrying of "church as entertainment" with "church as self-help." In an effort to be relevant to the culture, many churches—including some in the mainstream, but particularly the highly visible and baby-boomer-oriented megachurches—have become extreme examples of cultural accommodation and conformity. The consumer wants church to be exciting? Add drama, video, and contemporary music. People want churches to speak to contemporary issues? Preach sermons about what God would say to Bart Simpson. People want solutions to the tough problems of modern life? Create an image of a God who can be controlled through prayer. People want to feel better about themselves? Teach positive thinking.

As noted in the previous chapter, most churches of this type use the market-driven approach to worship as a means of attracting marginally interested visitors. The entertainment value and self-help orientation hide their evangelical piety and biblical seriousness. This type of church may be attractive to some mainstream Americans, but it is not likely to be the long-term answer for former establishment churches. What, after all, do mainstream churches have to disguise? Certainly not their openness and tolerance. Thus, mainstream churches that emulate evangelical megachurches are more likely to justify being labeled "spiritually vacuous" or "culturally accommodating" than the Willow Creeks and Calvary Chapels. Lacking ideological unity, an evangelical ethos, and a strong infrastructure of Bible studies and prayer groups, market driven mainstream churches are likely to be *nothing more* than "church as entertainment" and "church as self-help." Market-oriented evengelical churches typically are *much* more than that.

Third, we must realize that few mainstream churches will ever be aggressively evangelistic in the manner encouraged by most books on church growth. Based on poll data, mainstream members and marginal members, though they may desire intimacy with an immanent God, generally do not believe that an individual must "accept Christ as their personal Savior" in order to avoid going to Hell. Indeed, most of us don't believe in Hell as a literal place of divine retribution. And even those who *do* believe in such a Hell tend also to believe that God would not send good, moral persons there—whether they know Jesus or not. Salvation for mainstream Christians is a process that is nurtured within a community, local and global. It does not follow from a standardized formula. As a result, most mainstream Christians do not feel an urgency about evangelism, and large numbers even feel uncomfortable about using the word. "Evangelism" connotes door-to-door witnessing by Mormons, Jehovah's Witnesses, and other strongly doctrinal religious groups that are confident they have THE answer. Mainstream Christians may invite their friends to church, visit prospects, and even talk to others about their faith, but they won't do evangelism.[9] In other words, they will not try to *convert* anyone.

The answer to mainstream church growth is not found in imitating conservative Christianity or popular evangelicalism, nor is it found in imitating the popular culture. Mainstream church people cannot (and, given their theological inheritance, should not) accept the substance of such alternative streams of Protestant faith, nor their institutional style. Rather, the "answer" to mainstream church growth is to be found in liberal mainstream churches that are growing today.

Where Are We Growing?

Liberal church growth is not an oxymoron. Churches with liberal theological orientations are able to grow, despite the protestations of evangelical church growth practitioners.

Of the many types of growing mainstream churches, not all are liberal. Some, in fact, resemble "market-driven" evangelical churches, except that they are usually less dogmatic about their beliefs and somewhat more formal about worship. The fact that these churches exist does not contradict our assertions regarding the futility of imitating growing evangelical congregations. Churches of this type are not the answer for the mainstream, because few mainstream churches are able to change in this direction; thus the appeal of such congregations is limited.

Many other growing mainstream churches are in demographic settings where growth is easy. Most are solid, well-organized, and friendly, but otherwise unexceptional churches that would be stagnant or declining if they were located in rural areas, older suburbs, or the inner city. Church planners generally are not so naive about the growth of these congregations that they hold them up as models for other mainstream churches.

A third group of growing mainstream churches could be called "special purpose churches." Some congregations are reaching a unique market niche for which few churches are available. Gay/lesbian congregations, deaf congregations, churches for small racial/ethnic groups, and "radical/avant garde" congregations are examples of this type. They contribute to the potential growth of a denomination, but are too few to turn around the decline. They should, however, be encouraged in new-church development efforts.

The final group of growing mainstream churches provides a greater source of hope for denominations struggling with loss of identity and decline in members. These are the spiritually oriented mainstream churches. Such churches are unapologetically liberal and heavily involved in community ministry, with a clear focus on social justice. Yet the social and moral agenda of these churches is anchored in a deep, meaningful worship experience. We believe that churches of this type provide one "answer" to mainstream decline. They draw from the best of liberal mainstream tradition and provide a compelling alternative to the evangelical mode of congregational vitality.

The Spiritually Oriented Mainstream Church

The key element in a spiritually oriented mainstream church is worship. And the key element of worship in a spiritually oriented church is the expectation, the presumption, the surety, that God is present in the service and in the lives of anyone who is open to God's Spirit. As Leonard Sweet notes, this is not "conservative summer camp religion with its guitar-strumming, hand-clapping, bonfire toasty warmness. . . . Nor is [it] camp meeting religion, with its spiritual eruptions and irrational swoonings."[10] It is religious experience that welcomes the transcendent God in all God's mystery—without giving up reason or tradition.

As with all vital, growing churches, spiritually oriented congregations seem "different." These are not evangelical "celebrations," although there is some element of celebration in their worship. They would not be described as "fun," although participants probably have fun at their services. In worship style, most, but by no means all, are "liturgical" in worship style, sacramentally celebrating the mystery of God's presence. But their liturgy is not a matter of sleep-walking through ritual acts performed thousands of times before. Ritual is performed with reverence and expectation. The Bible, the reading of the Scriptures, the prayers, the celebration of the Eucharist, the liturgical dance, the passing of the peace, and the hymns—all are treated as if they are of utmost importance. This is not a worship technique. It is an attitude toward worship.

Churches with such a focus on worship are two giant steps beyond most mainstream churches, where "nobody talks about God" or where God is the God of politicians— a God mentioned only because one is expected to do so under certain circumstances. In growing spiritual churches, God is a God that is alive, a God that is, in fact, experienced and acknowledged to be present. This is not a distant or abstract God. It is a God that is both transcendent and immanent. Shirley Guthrie describes the seeming paradox of God's nearness and distance:

> *God is so transcendent that he can transcend even his transcendence!* He who is above space and time cannot be excluded from space and time as if they were impenetrable limits . . . . Without giving up but precisely by manifesting his transcendence, [God] is able to overcome the limits of space and time and to be present *in* them. . . . To put it in theological terms, God's transcendence means not only that [God] is a "hidden" God but that he is a God who can "reveal" himself.[11]

The Roman Catholic Church of St. Augustine and St. Paul in Washington, D.C. is a spiritual church. During one Sunday service, before the time for passing the peace (which lasts ten minutes or more), the priest said, "It would be a shame to leave here without knowing those around us." But then he paused and said slowly, "It would be a much greater shame to leave here without knowing God." This statement was followed by extended applause, as if people were telling God, who was in their presence, that they had no intention of leaving without knowing God.

The Federated United Church of Christ in Chagrin Falls, Ohio, is another church where the Spirit is alive. This church does not emphasize liturgy or the sacraments. In fact, services are often quite informal, even fun, particularly when children are included. Yet there is an expectancy in every service that God is there and cares about each person present. There is also a deep sense of responsibility that is part and parcel of their "liberal" approach to spirituality. This was seen clearly in a Sunday worship service organized around the birthday celebration of Martin Luther King, Jr. Early in the service, the congregation recited a "prayer of openness" from Ted Loder's *Guerrillas of Grace*:

> O Lord, we praise you for putting your presence in
>   our midst:
> in our darkness as in our light,
> in our struggles as in our ease,
> in winter as in spring.
> O God, in this hour, in this place,
> make us so aware of your grace
> that always and everywhere
> in gladness of heart and boldness of spirit,
> we move on in our darkness and share your light;
> grow in our struggles and be grown in our ease;
> be as honest as winter and as hopeful as spring;
> that your presence may become to us
> as real as the cold wind,
> as stark as the bare trees,
> as challenging as the ice,
> as beautiful as the snow,
> and as welcome as belonging with each other and you;
> through Jesus Christ, the Savior for all seasons.
>   AMEN![12]

After a short pause, the pastor of the church read Amos 5:12-15, 21-24—the key text in the "I Have a Dream" speech of Martin Luther King, Jr. This was followed by a litany in which the worship leaders and the congregation alternately read sections of "I Have a Dream." Later in the service, while wiping away his tears, the pastor recounted the past and present efforts of that church to combat racism, even in the midst of pressures to "leave well enough alone." It was a powerful, moving service, in which God's presence and the human response to God's presence were equally strong.

Donald Miller refers to this manifestation of spirituality as "religious experience." He defines it this way: "By 'religious experience,' I mean an experience of self-transcendence which is expressed in deeply felt ways that experientially conjure the feeling that one is not alone in this world, and that there is a sacred order that exceeds one's personal efforts at self- and world construction." [13] The church that "conjures" this experience for Miller is yet another spiritually oriented church: All Saints Episcopal Church in Pasadena, California.

It is difficult to adequately describe worship in a spiritually oriented church. Descriptions seem inadequate to capture the power, the depth of understanding, the sense of unity, and the palpable feeling of God's presence. There is a sense that "you had to be there." Like all experiences, feeling and sensing are primary; and like all powerful experiences, a great deal is lost in the translation when moving from what is felt to describing it with words.

This type of worship has nothing to do with contemporary, colloquial understandings of liberalism, *but it has everything to do with classical theological liberalism.* According to Peter Berger, "The turn from authority [of tradition or modernity] to *experience* as the focus of religious thought is, of course, by no means new. It has been the hallmark of Protestant theological liberalism at least since Friedrich Schleiermacher." [14]

For most spiritually oriented churches, the current liberal/conservative theological continuum has little meaning. If God is present, God is present, whether one takes a literal or symbolic interpretation of Scripture, whether one is pro-choice or pro-life. For this reason, spiritually oriented churches are able to attract a wide variety of members. Liberals are attracted to the openness and social activism that are usually present in such congregations—along with the spirit of worship and religious meaning. Conservatives are attracted to the serious treatment of Scripture—along with the spirit of worship and religious meaning. In the affirmation and celebration of God's presence in worship, there is unity and the realization that God may not be very concerned about our theological squabbles.

This type of church can be part of "the answer" for mainstream denominations because it is rooted in the classical liberal mainline tradition, and therefore does not require mainstream churches to adopt a "foreign identity." Spiritually stagnant mainstream churches must be revitalized, but what they can become is part of their heritage and latent in their present identities.

Growth and the Spiritual Church

What about growth? There is an adage that rings true: We should be less concerned about making churches full of people and more concerned about making people full of God.[15] The good news is that churches concerned about making people full of God are more likely to experience growth than mainstream churches that are concerned about growing (or not declining).

To grow and to continue growing, it is necessary for each mainstream church to become a vital *religious* institution, vibrant with the presence of God. It must develop a clear *religious* identity, a compelling *religious* purpose, and a coherent sense of direction that arises from that identity and purpose. According to Thomas Dipko, "If we cannot recover a sense of the numinous, of the sheer mystery of transcendence-in-our-midst, our worship will satisfy other needs perhaps, but not the spiritual hunger that makes authentic worship unique."[16] There must be religious "substance" to the mainstream church, or it will be unable to impart religious meaning.

This substance is nothing ethereal. It is quite concrete.

Church members must be able to sense the presence of God in worship and struggle openly with questions of ultimate meaning. These are not complex questions, but they are difficult to answer. Church members and unchurched persons want to know why God allows evil things to happen to good people, why a friend or relative died, and why so many people in the church don't act like Christians.[17]

The authority behind the answers to such questions, and what gives them plausibility, is not blind faith, religious tradition, the Word of God, or cold rationality. Religious interpretations of ultimate reality are not primarily rational, anyway, and the relativizations of modernity have undermined traditional bases of authority. Instead, our answers, our definitions of truth, are embedded in experience:

> Piety requires truth, but not necessarily in the old sense of absoluteness. The conviction that one has encountered God and heard his voice is not touched by the relativizations of historical consciousness. There are these encounters [with the supernatural] that carry with them an intrinsic conviction of truth. The individual can find certainty in this conviction. Even if he enters into the full gamut of historical and social-scientific relativizations, he can be confident that what has been experienced as truth by himself, and *what has proven itself truth in the lives of many other human beings, will never come to be seen as untruth.*[18]

The critical dimension of spiritually oriented worship is neither pure emotion nor intellect. It is a gut-level sense that God is here, active and alive.[19] This is another way of knowing—one that makes the emotion of religious experience feel less strange and the answers that churches provide seem more plausible.

The church that allows God to live in worship will not find it difficult to attract people. The experience of the presence of God is intrinsically attractive. Churches grow when they are vital organisms; when they have a core vitality that both attracts people and compels response— whether toward evangelism or social justice (or both).

Becoming a Spiritually Oriented Liberal Church

At an evangelism workshop, one participant told us the story of his conversation with a longtime pastor. He asked this retiring pastor to reflect on his thirty years in the ministry and tell him how things had changed. The pastor replied: "To do ministry today, it is necessary to be a person of faith. Thirty years ago, all it took was being a professional." The pastor also remarked that he was glad that he was getting out of the ministry now.

To lead a church that is spiritually alive, it is necessary for the pastor to be, first and foremost, a person of faith. Professional expertise alone will not suffice today. It is just too difficult for a pastor to *pretend* that he or she expects God to be present in worship, or to artificially create this expectation among the congregation. So the first step toward a spiritually vital congregation is that a pastor or the pastoral staff be (or become) people of faith. The next step is to take a different attitude into worship—an attitude of expectancy and seriousness about those things that are serious.

The third step is to work with lay leaders in rethinking the identity of the church. To ask, why are we here? What is the purpose of the church? What would God have us become? Answers to these questions will help church leaders begin to flesh out a new or renewed identity and vision for a congregation.

It is possible for a mainstream congregation to have a clear, compelling sense of identity. Such an identity might look something like this:

We are a church that is:

SPIRITUALLY ALIVE,
RADICALLY INCLUSIVE,
AND
JUSTICE-ORIENTED.

This identity, or mission statement, would help create a sense of purpose. It indicates a distinctively liberal mainstream identity that might help revitalize a church. And we maintain that revitalized churches tend to grow.

CHAPTER FIVE

The Denomination

HOW INSTITUTIONS HELP OR HURT

THE CONCEPT of denominational growth is meaningful only in a society where religious bodies compete with one another for adherents. This statement may seem obvious, but the element of competition is often missed. Our denominational society has created a unique and very level "playing field" for religious organizations. No state church is sanctioned. Being an American does not mean that one is automatically a part of any religion or any religious group. The very heart of American religious voluntarism is that one is free to choose. Religious institutions cannot take support for granted, either from the government or from the people.

The frontier character of early America and the lack of an established church helped to create a nation that resembled a "permanent mission field" for American church bodies. Successful religious groups were those that held onto their own, even as they sought to convert the multitudes of "lost" persons and bring them into the fold. As Roger Finke and Rodney Stark document in *The Churching of America*, these efforts were largely successful. Whereas in the late eighteenth century, only a small minority of Americans were counted as church members, by the early twentieth century, those affiliated with a church or synagogue were in the vast majority.[1]

Growth was relatively easy in a setting where large numbers of unchurched persons held traditional religious beliefs and population growth was rapid. People accepted the presuppositions of the church, even though most did not belong to a congregation. One major reason for the earlier low level of church membership was that churches were not available to a large proportion of a dispersed rural population. The rapid westward expansion of the nation had left the churches behind. But they soon caught up.

As the unchurched population became proportionally smaller and increasingly secularized in belief, growth became more difficult. Nevertheless, by the end of the nineteenth century, American society was more "churched" than most nations of the world. At this point, one might have expected American churches to shift from a conversionist orientation to simply being "the church" for the American population. Indeed, this was the direction taken by the mainstream. But it was not the course for all denominational families. The churching of America was accomplished by vital and aggressive religious movements which sought to convert the American population. They did not (and still do not) see the job as finished. Competition continues among churches, synagogues, mosques, temples, and covens, for the hearts, minds, and participation of the American public.

Conversionist religious movements grow rapidly among receptive populations in settings that allow religious competition. Religious movements may experience growth even where they are outlawed, although restrictions against open evangelism, rallies, publicity, congregating, and new church development tend to slow their expansion. But in a competitive environment, growth may be rapid until religious groups lose their movementlike quality and begin to act like established churches. Establishment-oriented groups may continue to grow, of course, but as we have seen in the case of the mainstream, they eventually become captive to the demographic trajectories of their constituencies. They also become increasingly susceptible to secularized indifference, on the one hand, and the more vitalized witness of religious movements on the other.[2]

It is not possible to be THE church *for* a pluralistic society that does not permit an established church. Established churches have a taken-for-granted quality. The church is an essential and habitual part of everyday life, and participation, therefore, is largely independent from the quality of worship, character of ministerial leadership, and outreach efforts.

Despite the impossibility, we have noted that mainstream denominations sought collectively and ecumenically to be "THE church" for American society. In order to do this, it was necessary for these church bodies to downplay doctrinal and other denominational distinctives, and to avoid proselytizing one anothers' members or adherents. Mainstream denominations recognized that they all were equally valid expressions of the Body of Christ. The unintended consequence was the public perception that "one church is as good as another," or "it doesn't matter which church you go to, just that you go to church." The impression was that mainstream churches believed "nothing in particular, and everything in general." Why go to church, when churches no longer seemed to know what they believe?

The fact that many diverse religious bodies coexist erodes any confidence that there is a single source of truth. It is difficult in such a context, therefore, for any religious body to claim, "this is the truth," with regard to ultimate questions. Denominationalism erodes religious plausibility structures—*particularly* for "culture affirming," ecumenically oriented institutions like mainstream denominations. Religious movements are able to succeed in this setting, however, because they create their own plausibility structures, which include compelling reasons for the movement's distinctive ethos. They are on the offensive, preaching, teaching, and living out definitions of reality that differ from those of the larger culture and from other religious bodies.

The intended direction of any religious movement is not to become a denomination. It is to be "THE church" for society, or for a subgroup of society. Movements have "the answer" or "the best answer," and typically seek to convert others to their viewpoint, or to withdraw from society. It is virtually impossible, of course, to convert enough people in American society in order to be "THE church." If the option of withdrawal is not chosen, societal and institutional realities pull a movement in the direction of denominationalism. A religious movement can "go with the flow," resist the pull, or withdraw from the larger society.

Religious movements tend to become sects (by withdrawing), or they become denominations that retain movement qualities. We call the latter "denominational movements." In settings of religious tolerance, the next stage is not that of the Troeltschian established "church," however. Denominational movements tend to become ecumenical religious bodies—denominations that try to act like THE church in a society in which it is not possible to be THE church. Groups that try to be THE church in a competitive environment inevitably stagnate, because their churches will never be taken for granted. Denominations are evaluated by what they provide for a religious consumer, in the context of the consumer's worldview. *Movements,* on the other hand, create a sense of necessity that allows their churches to be evaluated differently from churches in mainstream denominations.

From this perspective, *the only hope for mainstream growth is for mainstream church bodies to become more like movements and less like denominations.* Mainstream denominations cannot, however, become conservative, evangelical movements, any more than most mainstream churches can become conservative, evangelistically oriented congregations. The energizing vision of a new movement-like orientation for mainstream denominations is the experience of God, with the responsible, world-changing ramifications of that experience. A mainstream movement would not seek to convert people, but it would seek to change them—not through argument, proposition, or guilt, but through struggle and experience.

Having stated our primary conclusion, we now examine denominational growth in more detail. How denominations become more movementlike is developed further in our next chapter.

Denominational Growth and the National Context

Why do some denominations grow while others decline? Denominational growth is influenced by many factors, and one of these factors is the national context. Some historical periods are simply better for denominational growth—of all sorts. Other historical periods seem to favor only certain *types* of denominations.

For instance, Penny Long Marler and C. Kirk Hadaway show that a profound "period effect" has influenced all American denominations over the last several decades.[3] In the 1940s, rates of membership growth surged for all denominational families.[4] It was an atypical era in many respects. During this decade marriage rates climbed to record levels, and the baby boom began. Churches of all kinds capitalized on these changes by following new families to the suburbs and providing family-oriented programming.

The birth rate peaked in the early 1950s and began to decline before the end of the decade. This decline accelerated in the 1960s, as more women entered the labor force and oral contraceptives became available. Changing values regarding divorce, birth control, age of marriage, and optimal family size also contributed to declines in births. Smaller families, for example, were considered not only more practical from an economic perspective, but also a morally appropriate response to the "population explosion." The birth rate eventually dropped below replacement-level fertility for white Americans. Further, birth rates were especially low among *educated, middle-class white* people—the primary constituency of the mainstream.

Not surprisingly, rates of denominational membership growth dropped. As can be seen in Figure 5.1, the declines in average rates of membership change paralleled steep declines in the birth rate. The cultural ethos of the 1960s had an impact on denominations through the birth rate, but it also influenced denominational health in other ways. Churches and denominations were affected by changing values regarding church membership, church attendance, and the proper role of religious authority. Young adults, in particular, were more likely to question the value of religious institutions. They were less likely to participate in churches, and many dropped out of religion altogether.[5]

Declining rates of membership growth hit all denominational families in the 1950s and early 1960s. This fact did not register with denominational leaders at the time because net increases in membership remained substantial. In fact, as noted earlier, mainstream Protestant membership losses were seen as aberrations in the early years of decline. Serious efforts to understand the declines and reverse them were not organized until the mid-1970s—a decade after net losses began and at least two decades after growth rates began to decline.

FIGURE 5.1

Average Percent Change in Denominational Membership
and U.S. Birth Rate: 1950–1992

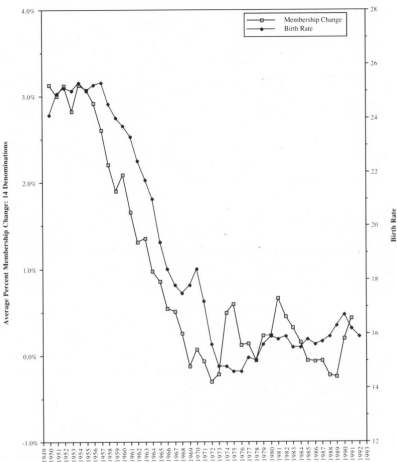

Because of close ties to mainstream culture, liberal mainstream denominations were hit harder by demographic and cultural change than the other denominational groups. Mainstream families had fewer children on average than conservative Protestant families. In addition, the children of mainstream families were less insulated from the changing cultural values and, therefore, more likely to drop out of the church once they became adults.

The demographic and cultural context make up part of the "playing field" for American denominations. Changes in this playing field affect everyone. The character of religious groups determines exactly how they are affected by the context, and how well they respond to changes in that context.

Denominational Growth Is Affected by Denominational Priorities and Actions

A shared national context explains parallel patterns of decline in rates of membership growth, but it does not explain continuing differences in the numerical "bottom line" between conservative and mainstream denominations. Conservative denominations may have experienced slower growth at the same time the mainstream was experiencing decline—but conservatives remained "in the black." This gap existed in the 1950s and persists today.

What denominations perceive as important, and the actions they take as a consequence, affect denominational membership trends. All other things being equal, mainstream denominations increase their chances for growth when they place a high priority on growth-related tasks. Mainstream denominations are affected by the culture and demographics, but all the evidence suggests that they would be declining less if they put more emphasis on outreach and new church development.

New church development and outreach are the "nuts and bolts" of denominational growth. Penny Long Marler and C. Kirk Hadaway show that new churches add to the growth of evangelical denominations and also help moderate the declines of the mainstream.[6] And as seen in the previous two chapters, evangelism (broadly defined) is the most important growth-producing action for congregations. New churches may be started or funded by denominational agencies, but effective recruitment effort is necessarily located at the congregational level. Nevertheless, denominations are able to encourage outreach as a denominational priority and assist local churches in the effort.

In the 1950s, rates of new church development were much higher than they are today. Starting churches was a major priority in all denominations, mainstream and evangelical. In addition, supporting evangelism was a central, high-profile denominational emphasis—receiving a large share of available program dollars in mainstream denominations. But mainstream denominational priorities changed, and denominational actions changed accordingly.

Cultural changes affect what people see as important. As shown by Bruce Greer, mainstream denominational priorities changed as the culture changed.[7] To some extent, new denominational priorities were necessary because of new socioeconomic realities. For example, new churches were more costly and more difficult to start in the 1970s. Nevertheless, most of the change in structure and policy can be traced to changing ideology. In the case of the American Baptist Churches, Greer notes that "evangelism that aimed solely for individual conversion was [seen as] too narrow and simplistic, failing to challenge all of society with the full claims of the gospel." Evangelism was redefined, and "a new church development famine ensued" as "other priorities concerned BNM [Board of National Ministries] staff, including the political and cultural upheaval of the nation."[8] We are not arguing that the change was inappropriate, but only that it had serious consequences for evangelism and membership growth.

In other mainstream denominations, evangelism and new church development retained their historic meaning but lost personnel, budget dollars, and organizational visibility. Other priorities—particularly those related to ecumenism, organizational restructuring, and social justice—came to the forefront. If programmatic emphases on growth-oriented procedures are related to denominational growth, then it is not surprising that mainstream denominations experienced difficulties.

Conservative denominations were not immune to the changes that affected the priorities of mainstream agencies, however. In several areas of the nation during the 1970s, the Southern Baptist Convention replaced traditional approaches to new church development with experimental techniques. Many other evangelical denominations increased emphasis on social-justice concerns. Nevertheless, these denominations never had a complete reorientation of their priorities. Traditional evangelism and new church development efforts continued to receive the lion's share of denominational mission funds.

Mainstream denominations have tried to reemphasize church growth in the 1980s and early 1990s. Yet Bruce Greer shows that even as these denominations were claiming evangelism as a priority, funding levels for church growth *did not* keep pace with inflation.[9] As a consequence, staff cuts reduced new church development efforts to minimal levels. Evangelism and new church development now compete with many other programs for money and clout. While evangelism and new church development programs are no longer considered quite so "embarrassing" (or irrelevant) by most mainstream denominational officials, these actions never regained their former prominence. In an era of slow population growth, high divorce rates, high building costs, and increased competition for time, denominations must work harder than ever to prevent membership loss. For the mainstream, church growth efforts to date have not been sufficient to reverse numerical decline.

Future prospects for renewed growth-related activities at the denominational level do not look promising. Financial problems continue to adversely affect the ability of mainstream denominational agencies to perform their traditional staff-driven programmatic functions. Even very loyal mainstream congregations are beginning to view contributions to national denominational offices as a waste of money, rather than as gifts to God. In fact, if present trends were to continue, gifts to denominational causes would reach zero by the middle of the next century.[10] Until mainstream denominations are revitalized, the energy necessary for evangelistic outreach (broadly defined) and new church development will be lacking.

Denominational Growth Is Affected by Denominational Character

The pattern of conservative denominational growth and mainstream decline has been constant since the mid-1960s. Even in the 1950s, as we show in chapter 1, evangelical denominations were experiencing more growth, on average, than mainstream denominations. Some of this growth differential was due to demographics. Indeed, evangelical denominations have higher birth rates, on average, than mainstream denominations.[11] Evangelical denominations also have younger constituencies, and some are heavily concentrated in growing areas of the nation. Yet these differences alone do not explain the numerical gap between conservatives and the mainstream. The mainstream, for instance, also loses in head-to-head competition in areas where the population is growing.

Mainstream and conservative denominations have different priorities, and these priorities affect rates of membership growth. What price are denominational executives (and their loyal congregations) willing to pay to alter their priorities? Are they willing to say, "We are going in the wrong direction," or, "Some of our established priorities and preoccupations are misguided"? Talk of "price" and "priorities" raises the issue of base commitments and ultimate concerns.

Why do some denominations engage in activities that produce growth, and others do not? Desire for growth may be part of the answer, but it does not explain the origin of that desire. Why might a denomination desire to grow—other than to retain staff positions at the national level and increase the flow of program dollars? Such motivations inspire no one. Clearly, there must be a commitment to "share the good news," whatever the specific content of the "good news" might be. In order to be evangelistic and to "plant" a lot of churches, a denomination must have an identity and a vision that will enable these activities to seem reasonable and compelling.

For mainstream denominations, evangelism and new church development seem neither reasonable nor compelling. This is not the case for denominations that retain the characteristics of movements, however. Goals are widely shared and commitment is high. Leaders and members believe that they have a mission to convert people to Christ, and they feel a compelling urgency to be about that task. They are willing to pay the price.

In denominational movements, growth-related actions are less affected by the contextual situation, because great efforts will be made without regard to the appropriateness of such actions. If the times (or the territory) discourage proselytizing, denominational movements are usually up to the task. Whether twenty or a hundred calls are needed to "harvest a lost soul," they will be made. Whether or not a neighborhood is demographically favorable for growth, a new church is just as likely to be planted. Despite their age, many of these denominations still call themselves "movements."

High levels of commitment and ideological fervor tend to encourage volatility. In fact, churches in denominational movements, such as the Assemblies of God, have a "boom or bust" quality. Large numbers of churches are growing, but large numbers also are declining. And unlike mainstream or conservative denominations, the Assemblies of God have few churches that are stable in membership.[12]

In some ways, older conservative denominations resemble denominational movements, and in some ways they are very different. Groups like the Southern Baptist Convention and the Lutheran Church, Missouri Synod, have large numbers of stable, plateaued congregations. In this respect, these traditionalist conservative denominations look more like the mainstream. One feature shared by groups like the Assemblies of God and Southern Baptists, however, is the fact that much of their growth comes from large entrepreneurial, independent-minded congregations.[13] These congregations are localized expressions of movement orientation. Mainstream denominations have few congregations of this type.

The Issue Is Identity

Growing denominations tend to be ideologically conservative. Yet the key to their growth or "social strength" is not conservatism, strictness, tension with the culture, or high demands, *per se*. The key is a strong sense of identity and a compelling vision. Religious social movements want to transform the lives of their adherents. They do this by presenting a redefinition of reality, complete with a compelling vision of how people should relate to God and to one another. The movement proclaims that "we have the truth, we have the answer," and the members feel it is their mission to bring the vision into reality.

In describing "high demand" religion, Laurence Iannaccone states, "Potential members are forced to choose: participate fully or not at all. The seductive middle-ground of free riding and low participation is eliminated."[14] This is largely true, but it misses the point. Potential converts are welcomed by movements, and as a result, movements often have many more *temporary* "free riders" than do established denominations. Yet long-term status as a bystander or free rider makes little sense for someone who is confronted by the identity, vision, and mission of a dynamic social movement. Ultimately, one must become a convert—a "true believer"—or else reject the movement and its vision.

Strong churches are demanding, but they are not strong *because* they are demanding. This change of emphasis, from the demands of a denomination to its *character*, or *strength*, eliminates the dilemma created by Dean Kelley and perpetuated by Roger Finke and Rodney Stark.[15] That is, what do less strict and less demanding denominations *do* in order to become "strong churches" and grow? Do they try to add strict rules of conduct and other demands? This is the implication of what could be called the "strict church thesis." But adding demands is counterproductive, without a prior change in the essential character of a religious institution.

Can a church that demands little of its members become a more vital institution by increasing its demands? Obviously not. Efforts by the Roman Catholic Church to do just that in the United States only drive away its marginal members and alienate many committed Catholics. Given the choice between fewer demands and more demands, most people will choose fewer demands and resist the imposition of more. A religion can become more demanding and avoid decline only if its members first accept the necessity, or what might be called the "naturalness," of the demands. In other words, what may be demands to an outsider are reasonable expectations to a participant. According to Luther P. Gerlach and Virginia H. Hine, movement adherents "emphasize the effortlessness of the desired behavior. They consider moral behavior a consequence of the religious experience, not a prerequisite or social duty."[16]

Churchlike institutions must be revitalized before they can be "strong" enough to make demands. But *can* such institutions be revitalized, or must they be replaced by competing organizations which already have the character necessary to make demands? Our answer is that revitalization is possible, but very difficult. Many historical examples of revitalized institutions can be listed, although the ideological content of some should not be emulated. Several come immediately to mind: the Red Guard in China, monastic movements in western Europe, the Inquisition, and perhaps the Great Awakenings. The recent takeover of the Southern Baptist Convention is another, more limited, example of an ideological "centering" of an increasingly "churchlike" denomination.

We are not lifting up these movements and others like them as examples of "healthy movements." They are mentioned only because they are examples of revitalization from within. Leaders and converts arose largely from within the established institutions, rather than coming in from outside. A compelling vision for change emerged. And it was this self-validating vision, based on a symbolic and behavioral restructuring, that led to the kind of heightened commitment that could carry the burden of demands. The demands could not be imposed, nor would they be accepted by anyone other than "true believers."

Strong denominations—those that are vital or have been revitalized—*appear* to be strict because they are demanding. Most are conservative. Yet we maintain that neither strictness nor conservatism are necessary components of a dynamic religious organization. Instead, the vitality comes from the vision, and from living out the dream.

The Dilemma of Liberal Church Growth

The Episcopal Church and the Unitarian Universalist Association should *not* be growing, if the strict church thesis is correct. Yet these presumably "secularized" denominations grew during the last several years, while the rest of the mainstream declined. Another problem for the thesis is the finding by Wayne Thompson, Jackson Carroll, and Dean Hoge that "liberal" Presbyterian churches are more likely to grow than are conservative Presbyterian churches.[17]

Why would two of the most theologically liberal denominations in America grow, when more moderate denominations are in serious decline? And why would congregations that are theologically liberal experience more growth than conservative churches? In fact, *they should not,* if theological conservatism must accompany strong identity, vision, purpose, and a demanding faith. But if the specific content of the vision is irrelevant to a coherent religious identity, then conservatism is an unnecessary component. As we have argued in the previous chapter, it is possible for a *liberal* or a nonideological congregation to have a strong identity, vision, and purpose. Here we suggest that the same is true for a mainstream denomination, without becoming conservative, in the American evangelical sense. We also believe that such a denomination is quite likely to grow, particularly if members are encouraged to share their version of the "good news" with others. In doing so, it may appear more demanding than the mainstream denominations of today, but it will not *seem* more demanding to its members.

CHAPTER SIX

Mainstream Movements

NEARLY EVERYONE AGREES that mainstream denominations are in the midst of an identity crisis, largely resulting from the "disestablishment" of this stream of Protestantism from its status as the unofficial "Church" of American society. In denomination after denomination, people ask: "What are we about?" "What is our purpose?" "What is the glue that holds us together?"[1] Articles and books discuss "Protestant identity in a post-Protestant age" and "the post-denominational church," with a clear sense about what was lost, but with uncertainty about what we have become.[2]

Several years ago, in an address titled, "So how do we turn things around?" William McKinney suggested that these identity struggles were a new development for the mainline, or "oldline":

> For most of their history in America, the oldline churches were spared the difficult task of defining themselves theologically or justifying their place in the culture. That they knew what they stood for and that they belonged could be assumed.[3]

Descriptions of the "Protestant establishment" often give the impression of a monolithic institution whose values formed the kernel of American culture. Indeed, there was a sense that American values were Protestant values. In an operational sense, however, the Protestant establishment was composed of distinct activist denominations on parallel missions. They were strong, vital, optimistic organizations that tried to effect change, and they thought they knew how to do it better than anyone else. From the emergence of denominationalism shortly after the American revolution, until perhaps 1830, the primary goal of the Protestant establishment was to "save souls" and make America a "Christian nation." In that era, all of us were "evangelicals."

The task of Christianizing America was largely accomplished prior to the Civil War, and, according to Martin Marty:

> The Protestant leaders often looked at the empire which they had created and called its design very good . . . . But the details of America were not perfect, and evangelicals by nature could not be content with less than ideals of perfection . . . . In a progressive spirit and with revivalist fervor they set out to improve the moral situation and to engage in mopping up operations against the residual forces of evil in their empire.[4]

The transforming character of the Protestant establishment was strong. These denominations intended to *remake* American society into something resembling the "Kingdom of God" on earth. They felt confident that they knew what was right for America and also had a keen sense of responsibility for its direction. Consequently, they were not hesitant about exercising whatever influence they could muster.

An element of passivity also was present in the mainstream constituency, however, and at times this restrained the activist impulse. Throughout the nineteenth century and into the twentieth, the Protestant establishment alternated between activism and self-satisfied complacency. Indeed, during the 1880s, J. B. Harrison suggested that "the real religion of the people" had become "a decorous worldliness." Protestantism represented a status quo that was uneasy with its own success.[5]

Beginning in the 1920s, but even more strongly following the end of World War II, churches in the ecumenical branch of evangelical Protestantism, what we now call the mainstream, began to act less like distinct denominations on parallel missions and more like a single Established Church, with a highly developed collective sense of responsibility for "its" culture. Unfortunately, the increasing secularism and pluralism of American society meant that the society no longer *belonged* to the mainstream, and even the mainstream's own constituency often questioned the continual rhetoric of transformation.

The mainstream's ability to "run things," or even to *help* run things, is long gone. The activist impulse is still there, of course, and can be observed in the efforts of national agencies and special-interest groups to promote social change. But hardly anyone is paying attention. Few people at the grassroots level really care anymore what the national religious leaders or national conventions, assemblies, and synods say. What one leader says is contradicted by another, and there is a growing feeling among Americans that it is inappropriate to voice opinions born out of religious conviction. Efforts by mainstream, evangelical, and fundamentalist Christians to transform society, whether by political action or aggressive evangelism, are seen as demagoguery and evidence of religious intolerance.

Having given up on efforts to transform the American population through evangelism, and having lost the ability to reform American society through social activism, what now is the purpose of denominational boards, agencies, and instrumentalities? Local churches look at them and wonder. Boards and national agencies make futile efforts to change society through actions that are seen as either extremist or irrelevant. These futile efforts include social activism *and* evangelism. Sending denominational bureaucracies money to "work their own agenda" is viewed by many churches as a waste. Denominational structures, born out of and energized for nearly a hundred years by an activist impulse, had lost, at least in their members' eyes, their reason for being.

These embattled national denominational agencies symbolize denominational culture. So is there any wonder that we are experiencing a collective identity crisis? It is our view that until mainstream denominations reestablish their respective identities, purpose, and vision, they will continue to drift and decline. And unless mainstream denominational agencies have a definite role in this revitalization, the effort will fail.

Reforming Mainstream Identity

Mainstream Protestantism must stop trying to be the established church for the cultural center. The cultural center no longer exists. American society is a pluralistic conglomeration of individuals and competing subcultural groups, loosely bound by pragmatic realities and secularized morality. The former mainstream establishment is one of many voices seeking to influence the direction of the whole. But in its continuing social activism and efforts to reform America, the mainstream has become captive to the more liberal, secular elements of society, groups that share many of our goals, but not our religious values.

Mainline Protestantism should take advantage of the pluralistic character of American society and withdraw from direct participation in America's liberal/conservative "culture war."[6] We are in an age where communists are the conservatives in the former Soviet Union. Being "progressive" or "liberal" has lost much of its meaning. Perhaps as mainstreamers, we do not want to be dogmatic and intolerant, the charges we cast at fundamentalists. But we also do not need to be the antithesis of fundamentalism. We can be . . . well, different—not liberal, not conservative. We can ignore the continuum and be something else.

The central element to a revitalized mainstream, as we have argued for congregations and, we believe, which also is true for denominations, is the reclamation of religious experience and spirituality, to let the tangible presence of God back into our churches and national structures. It is to be the Body of Christ:

> The primary [role] of the church is not to be an aesthetic, cultural movement. The primary [role] of the church is not to be an intellectual or missionary movement. The primary [role] of the church is not to be a political or social justice movement. The primary purpose of the church is not to change the world, or to preach to the world, or to serve the world. The primary function of the church, from which stems all other[s], is to be the body of Christ—quite sacramentally, Christ enfleshed, incarnated, embodied in presence and in power.[7]

To be the Body of Christ, the church must create spiritual communities where Christ's Spirit is allowed to live and breathe, and so to animate its many members. But more than just creating and nurturing spiritually oriented communities, national denominational structures themselves must promote, organize, and embody worshipful celebrations of the experience and presence of God. Doing so should be the primary business of denominational meetings. And as we have noted previously, this is more an attitude and expectation than a technique or method. Perhaps it could be called faith.

A denomination that is spiritually alive expects and

makes room for the expression of religious experience in corporate worship, and in the private communion of its members with God. In fact, the purpose of all worship, public or private, shifts from its current overemphasis on cognitive instruction, esthetic inspiration, and cultural diversity, to communion with God. This is not, however, religious experience "divorced from reason and restraint." Rather, this is the experience of the presence of God, infused with human meaning as interpreted through reason, Scripture, and the historical witness of the church. The human "experience of God's love, forgiveness, and presence in the liberal tradition is not something irrational, disruptive, or beyond control."[8] Reason permits a fuller and more mature expression of one's emotional response to the living God.

From Denomination to Movement

If the mainstream is to have a vital future, it must be vitalized through the experience of God's presence—becoming less like denominations and more like movements. A critical part of our suggestion is that mainstream denominations must have something distinct, something valuable and meaningful that is not available from other institutions in society or from the culture at large. A movement is a "cause" in which people can believe. It is naturally in tension with the larger society. Within a secular society—one that seeks to function without God—the churches' celebration of the experience of God is a dramatically distinct and sufficient source of meaning, through which a movementlike structure may be energized.

Although spiritually oriented worship and faith-oriented lives will mark the church as distinct from the secular society, sectarian withdrawal into an insulated subcultural world is *not* a realistic option for mainstream members. That is, they will continue to spend the vast majority of their time "in the real world," rather than in the church or with church people; and they will continue to live in the world, not as "resident aliens" (to use a currently popular image), but rather as full participants. Given this fact, the mainstream has three basic options: (1) concede the world to the secular; (2) bring the secular into the church; or (3) claim the secular as a God-given arena for living out one's faith. The first two approaches have led to many of the mainstream's current troubles.

Therefore, we believe that one characteristic of the mainstream-as-movement will be a return to a highly developed sense of lay vocation. If the vitalizing experience of God in worship is to be carried forth into daily life, the church must help members affirm the "sacred" value of faithfully performing "secular" tasks.

Another necessary characteristic of our vision of the mainstream-as-movement, closely related to the last, is the balancing of criticism with affirmation. It is impossible to reinvigorate a sense of lay vocation or to reclaim a faith-driven social activism if the fundamental attitude of the church toward the concrete, contemporary, everyday "secular" world that is inhabited by our members (or members to be) is one of alienation, fear, or avoidance. In *The Church Confident,* Leander Keck makes a similar argument in his call for a "hermeneutic of affirmation" as an essential ingredient in mainstream renewal.[9] Keck applies his hermeneutic of affirmation primarily toward a positive recovery of the church's historical witness. To it, we would add the need for the recovery of a realistic, yet hopeful and affirming attitude toward the world.

Retreat from "the world" is unnecessary (and counterproductive) in the midst of a strategic offensive, to use what might be considered overly militaristic language. The mission of the church is to give coherent form, visible expression, and meaningful interpretation to religious experience. This can be done *without* constructing strong social boundaries. By embracing what is good about the culture and attending to the spiritual needs of the presently churched and the unchurched, the focus of a denomination-as-movement is on spreading the Word and living out the vision, rather than on consolidating what remains, or on reviving a fondly remembered past within a tightly bounded social group. A successful movement co-opts the culture by recasting accepted cultural understandings in a new, dynamic form. And if the vision is radical enough, it may be possible to break out of the long-standing "sect-to-church" cycle of cultural accommodation. A transformed church can be reintegrated into society and become a more natural part of everyday life. Routinization is inevitable; accommodation is not.

A Grassroots Beginning

If the future of the mainstream is for each national church body to become less like a denomination and more like a movement, the next question is: "How might this happen?" It is easy for mainstream leaders to assume that such a transformation can occur only spontaneously, through an internal revival or a sudden surge of religious interest among the American people. Whether attribution for this change is given to God's Spirit or to collective behavior, revivals and other social movements are often seen as capricious events that cannot be engineered.

There is some truth to assumptions regarding the spontaneity of movement formation. So many factors are involved—receptivity, precipitating events, leadership, ideology, cultural constraints—that intentional efforts to transform institutions into movements may seem futile.

We believe, however, that current social conditions are favorable for movement formation among spiritually interested Americans who hold liberal theological and social values. In other words, a receptive population exists within mainstream churches and among persons who are currently marginal to the church, those whom Penny Long Marler and C. Kirk Hadaway call "Marginal Members" and "Mental Affiliates."[10]

Many people are interested in spiritual matters, but many also feel uncomfortable with the dominant institutional expressions of religion in American society. Churches provide little that interests such individuals. Our churches are seen as either spiritually dead, socially intolerant, or irrelevant to modern life. Alternative expressions of religion, such as New Age spirituality, lack stable institutionalized forms. A religious void, or hunger, exists in this nation that has helped expand the ranks of persons who retain only tenuous connections to institutionalized religion. We believe that many Americans would resonate with the type of welcoming, spiritually oriented approach to worship that we outline.

What we are missing is charismatic leadership and a new type of church—a nonjudgmental, inclusive church with a vibrant faith, identity, and vision. Leaders are needed to articulate the vision for such a church and to spread the word. Congregations are needed to demonstrate the reality of the message and to provide mass support for the movement.

A critical question remains, however. What is the *source* of leadership for a revitalized mainstream movement?[11] Optimally, leadership for a successful movement should come from within the current elite structure of the institution to be revitalized. Such leaders already have personal influence and political power. If a compelling new vision for change emerges from key denominational leaders, transformation could occur rapidly, and with minimal institutional conflict. But this scenario seems unlikely for mainstream Protestant denominations.

Mainstream church leaders are not charismatic figures, by and large. They are persons with integrity, but they are more comfortable with consensus-building than at exercising visionary leadership. They do not, for the most part, have broad-based networks of loyal "clients" or "followers" among mainstream pastors, seminary faculty, and other church leaders who look to them for political and ideological cues. And they do not have the political capital to survive the attacks that would come if they tried to transform their fragmented denominations into unified movements. But following the lead of Mikhail Gorbachev in precipitating a second Russian revolution, perhaps they should try. After all, *glasnost* (new thinking) must always precede *perestroika* (restructuring), and current denominational leadership could at least begin the process of radically rethinking mainstream identity.

Under present circumstances, the leadership for revitalization is most likely to emerge among respected pastors who represent, but are not captive to, the cultural core of their denominations, and who are known as persons of faith. In other words, potential leaders probably will be pastors who are not perceived as representing the far left or right of a denomination, much less a "don't ask, don't tell" attitude toward God. Rather, the leaders will be spiritual persons who are disconnected from the current ideological debate. In fact, they will help transcend such debates by embodying a new ideological and behavioral synthesis that is attractive to (most, not all) denominational "liberals" and "conservatives."

There will be political conflict associated with any such movement, of course. Much of the "heat" will come from a denominational hierarchy that naturally resists fundamental change and typically attempts to portray reform movements as either too reactionary or too hungry for power. Under some circumstances, denominational elites may "jump on board" with movement leaders in an effort to co-opt the movement and perhaps control it. Under other circumstances, denominational elites will join the movement in a true partnership of purpose.

Unfortunately, current revitalization efforts in the mainstream only echo the liberal/conservative dichotomy that currently divides the American public. Some mainstream grassroots leaders want to pull their denominations toward evangelicalism, to engineer a type of revitalization effort similar to that which is currently transforming the Southern Baptist Convention. Others emphasize a less evangelical, but equally conservative, "confessional" ideology. As we have already indicated, neither approach will work. Among mainstream people, there are not enough potential "troops" with properly conservative worldviews to sustain such movements.

The progressive impulse is strong among mainstream Christian leaders. So any revitalization effort must be seen as moving forward, rather than as reclaiming the past. Yet movement toward increased relativism and contemporary liberalism is not the answer either. Any new vision for the mainstream must be a synthesis that is seen as progressive, but as neither liberal nor conservative, in the current meaning of these terms. It must be different, in a postmodern sense, and distinct from the linear liberal/conservative continuum.

As we see it, the pastors, local church leaders, and seminarians who will form the leadership core of a denominational revitalization movement will begin as an informal collection of individuals who share a common understanding of the flaws of the current system, but a deep commitment to the heritage it represents. Out of this group will emerge the awareness that we already have the solution among us. It is visible in the way spiritually oriented churches are currently doing worship and ministry. The next step is articulation of a vision that captures the new approach and allows it to be transmitted to others.

The movement would thus begin as a *network* of committed reformers, with one or more charismatic leaders and a set of churches where the new identity and vision are modeled. They will then expand the network, sharing the vision, spreading the theological understanding, and telling the story of churches that embody the essence of the cause.

Movement Structure

The institutional structure for a denomination-as-movement is not one of our major concerns, because this is not primarily a structural solution. The mainstream has more than enough institutions and agencies, books of discipline, and established procedures to "get the job done" from an organizational perspective. What we need are new ways of thinking about the structure and its purpose. Structural forms are only the regular channels through which the core (or defining) "work" of a church (the sharing of ritual, the communication of symbolic meaning, and the operation of social networks of fellow "believers") gets done. Changing the structure, even in very rational ways, is unlikely to improve the quality of the "work."

Primary attention should be given to the experience of God and to the symbolic meaning systems that give birth to it and make it interpretable. When, or if, a movement emerges, it will begin with a dynamic, free-flowing, web-like structure—until we begin to add rational, centralized organizational components. This should be resisted. We should allow the structure of a denomination-as-movement to remain "movementlike" for as long as possible.

We envision such a movement as a decentralized partnership of churches, judicatories, denominational agencies, independent parachurch organizations, and individuals, connected through a nonhierarchical network of intersecting lines of relationships. As Luther Gerlach and Virginia Hine demonstrate, the modern social movement is a dynamic, evolving entity, which grows in spite of the diversity, segmentation, and "internecine dogfighting" typical of most.[12] Like a river without a dam, a movement grows on its own by extending the web at any segment of its often ill-defined boundary. Control is not the issue; the issue is doing whatever is necessary to be faithful (and helpful) to "the cause" and its goals.

Ironically, given the paradigm shifts in the global economic village, this is also the structural form that more and more business consultants are advocating as necessary for competitive effectiveness in today's rapidly changing and highly diverse global marketplace—that is, if they are to successfully transform themselves from "modern" organizations to "postmodern" organizations.

In a weblike structure, geographically dispersed units are tied together, not through any central point, but directly, through intersecting lines. And indeed, this is the very essence of emerging electronic communication—a reality that the business world is using to make decentralization work for it, and which we believe the church could use as well. In such a structure, national denominational agencies can become equal partners with congregations, local judicatories, and parachurch organizations, without a monopoly of communication leading to a monopoly of power.

That denominational agencies could become true partners with other church bodies assumes, of course, that denominational agencies and offices have legitimate and important functions appropriate to their national level of organization. We believe this to be true. Some are purely instrumental, building on the advantages of scale that often accrue to national levels of organization. Other functions are symbolic, and even more important than instrumental functions, because the primary "business" of denominational structures is to symbolize a denomination's distinct *religious* identity. We also believe that national structures should have primary (but not exclusive) responsibility for maintaining/remembering/affirming the denomination's historical witness.

Revitalized mainstream Protestant denominations must become progressive, decentralized movements:

> *Communions of affirmation, memory, and partnership that welcome all to experience God's life-changing presence and to celebrate Scripture, the historical witness of the church, and reason, as guides for making God's presence alive, in themselves and in the world.*

Already, some denominations are in the midst of "deconstruction," as they downsize and "spin off" responsibility for certain activities to judicatories and parachurch organizations. In addition, independent networks of churches are forming across the face of mainstream Protestantism—often without regard to denominational boundaries. For example, two hundred pastors of tall-steeple churches have established a mission network that is separate from any denomination or traditional ecumenical structure (such as the National Council of Churches). As another example, the Leadership Network, funded by the Buford Foundation, is helping sponsor the Teaching Church Network, in which churches will mentor one another. In other words, traditional denominational relationships and power structures are being replaced by new, weblike structures, even without the unifying movement that we envision. What is lacking, of course, is the ethos and energy to join these networks and institutions into such a movement. Only then would the mainstream stop meandering and find its new course.

The fact that emerging new networks already include several denominational streams presents the possibility that new denominations will not look much like the old. This may be true, but we do not envision the end of denominationalism. In fact, we think that movements will revive denominational spirit, as each church body begins to reestablish its identity and develop a unique approach to spiritually oriented worship.

The Role of Denominational Leadership

Current national leadership in mainstream institutions is distracted by countless "brush fires," pulled in a thousand directions by special-interest groups, burdened by financial woes, and attacked by radical voices on both left and right. Serious efforts by national agencies to support a grassroots movement are unlikely, except by individual national staff members who "catch the vision," connect to the reform network, and do what they can to work within the system for change.

Perhaps the most helpful thing a national staff person can do at the present time is to assist in the development of a network of spiritually oriented congregations that already have the type of identity and movement character that is required. And once the movement begins, denominational leaders could help spread the vision and awareness of the movement. They can produce resources, organize conferences, and establish new congregations around the vision.

The very last thing to encourage is that the existing structures of denominations organize committees to study these issues. That would kill a movement before it begins.

CHAPTER SEVEN

Growth Futures

PERHAPS YOU CAN REMEMBER, as we do from our churched youth, using your entwined fingers to act out the words: "Here is the church. Here is the steeple. Open the door, and see all the people!" Perhaps you have noted, as we have, that the reality of brimming pews is not often seen anymore in mainstream churches.

For more than a quarter century, mainstream Protestantism has been losing members, and during this entire period, every invigorated call for evangelism has been met with an even more vigorous rejoinder that church growth is *not* the point. If you are one of those readers who starts with that conclusion, you may be chagrined to learn that *we agree that church growth is not the point.* Vital witness, in response to the affirming experience of the presence of God, is the point. Unlike most critics of the church growth movement, however, we find it a strange twist of logic to use membership declines as a validation of the presumed vitality of the status quo. But at least such critics have engaged the debate. Far more troubling to us is most church leaders' silence with regard to the declines. It is a disturbing parallel to the "don't ask, don't tell" approach toward God found in all too many mainstream churches.

Mainstream Protestantism has always walked precarious fine lines—between human responsibility and dependence on God; between individual freedom and a collective sense of mission. In accepting partnership with God, we also burden ourselves with our own responsibility as God's witnesses. And this responsibility, combined with our sense of mission to all of God's creation, should caution us to worry when a significant part of creation seems unresponsive to our witness. More than a quarter century of membership declines, we believe, is more than sufficient cause for worry, and more than sufficient warrant for honest self-examination.

In that spirit, this book has attempted a searching analysis of the mainstream's own responsibility for the declines. Church growth may not be the point, but we believe the declines do, in fact, carry a symptomatic message, which we have sought to diagnose with hard data. Building from the diagnosis, and identifying latent resources for change within our historical identity, we have risked voicing a proposal for renewal—one that calls for new networks, which could shift us away from survivalist mentalities.

The diagnosis is necessarily complex, but not overly surprising or difficult to comprehend. And it includes many rays of hope. But a "faithful fix"—for mainstream congregations and national denominational structures—remains a challenge. It is a challenge not only of imagination, but more critically, it is the challenge of embodying change— the challenge of letting go of comfortable habits and familiar patterns, in the anticipation of receiving and responding to God in a "new" way.

The reasons for the mainstream's decline are, indeed, complex. And many of the challenges we have identified are, for all practical purposes, beyond our control:

• Birth rates among our traditional, white, educated, affluent constituency are the lowest of any denominational family in the United States—so low that even if every child of every current member were to join one of our churches, we still would not have sustained growth.

- Mainstream congregations are concentrated in regions of the nation with low population growth (but as a caution against using this as an excuse, it must be added that we're not growing even in the South or West).
- The sweeping, baby-boomer-driven value changes of the 1960s have permanently replaced "church as obligation" with "church as choice" as the sociocultural norm.
- The increasing racial, ethnic, lifestyle, value, and religious diversity of American society has shattered any lingering possibility that the mainstream can be the religious establishment.

Many of the obstacles to growth which we have identified, however, are of our own doing, and therefore are within our power to change:

- We have embraced human agency while forgetting our own dependence on God—which is to say that we are more comfortable seeing one another than seeing God; and when we do invoke God's name, it's more often than not for our own self-gratification.
- We have seemingly abandoned the intensity of religious experience for a reasoned civility; and in overstepping our theological instinct for tolerance, we have made pluralism our latest "ism."
- We have stretched our championing of individual freedom to the breaking point of collective mission, and in doing so, the notion of congregations as moral communities has given way to religious service stations, filling individual needs.
- We have lost confidence in who we have been, allowing the voices of alienating criticism to hold sway over those of an affirmative realism.
- We have let our affirmation of the priesthood of all believers and local empowerment be undermined by the "efficiencies" of bureaucratic centralization.

If the diagnosis were to end here, the future would indeed look bleak. But there are rays of hope:

- A resurgence of interest in spirituality is evident, both in our churches and among the unchurched.
- Church participation has increased among baby boomers.
- Increasing numbers of genuinely liberal and vital congregations do exist, to which we can look for guidance.
- Emergent communication technologies free us from the heretofore seductive and corruptible pull of the efficiencies of bureaucratic centralization.
- A deepening sense of crisis pulls at least some of our leaders beyond avoidance or cynicism.
- Thousands of congregations and millions of members retain their loyalty and mission, even as they see the future but dimly.
- A deepening reservoir of recruitment techniques that work is available.

So what about a "faithful fix"—one that is honest about the diagnosis and realistic about the mainstream's liberal theological heritage, with its often-complacent middle-to-upper-middle-class constituency? Honesty about the diagnosis leads us to believe that merely adding any of the now proven recruitment techniques to the typical mainstream congregation's existing program arsenal won't help much toward achieving sustained membership growth. Indeed, the primary message we discern from the mainstream declines is that our churches lack a compelling *reason* for reaching out to unchurched and underchurched Americans. Nothing short of a pervasive revitalization, therefore, will suffice.

In our judgment, the mainstream's historical grounding in the worldliness of the middle class, and its historical grounding in the liberal theological tradition, preclude conservative, evangelical routes to revitalization. Rather, we argue that the route to vitality is emergent in the increasing number of mainstream congregations that have their grounding in spiritually oriented worship, contagious with the expectation, the presumption, the surety that God is present and active.

The centerpiece of spiritually oriented worship, as researchers have observed it, and as congregations articulate their own self-understanding of it, is the affirming celebration of the experience of the presence of God. In contrast to mainstream temptations toward seeking ultimate authority and validation in either reasoned doctrine or reasonable behavior, spiritually oriented worship asserts the primacy of the experience of God. In contrast to mainstream temptations toward either sectarian withdrawal, or the emotive self-gratification of worship as entertainment and theology as self-help, the experience of God compels a moral response to God's gift of all creation. And in contrast to dogmatic conversionism, a grounding in the experience of God balances the urgency of action with the necessity of openness.

The latter point is perhaps the most difficult to comprehend. Yet it is intrinsic to an incarnate faith. It hinges on two confessions. One is the finitude (dare we say, "fallenness") of humanity. The second is that while the experience of God is both self-validating and compelling, the content of the compelled response is not self-interpretive. The response is left to human agency, so that by applying all the resources of reason, Scripture, and the historical witness of the church, we will be shaped and infused with the cognitive necessities humans need for meaning. And precisely because this interpretive infusing of meaning and direction is a human production, it is subject to the limitations of human finitude and therefore requires openness. Indeed, this openness is the heart of what traditionally has been called "the Protestant principle," which stands both as one of the greatest strengths and one of the greatest liabilities of our liberal theological heritage.

The strategic implications of choosing the worshipful affirmation of the presence of God as the route to mainstream revitalization are many and varied, and beyond full elaboration in this book. We have tried, nevertheless, to suggest what strike us as critical first steps, both for congregations and for national denominational structures. Perhaps most important, these include:

• Reclaim the worshipful affirmation of the experience of God as the primary (not the only, but the primary) "business" of both congregations and denominational structures, and relatedly, reassert the charisma of drawing others into this experience as the primary requisite of church leadership—lay and ordained.
• Risk the closure required to infuse our response to God with human purpose, while remembering that such closure is but a momentary "best effort" of the human imagination.
• Engage the world with an affirmative realism, both through rekindling a progressive spirit toward social justice and ministry, and, even more important, through re-encapsulating the everyday "work" of everyday persons with a renewed sense of Christian vocation.
• Structure our denominational relationships and our networking partnerships with other allies, in ways that do not, whether by intent or through naivete, confuse unity with uniformity, connectedness with centralization, or empowerment with dominance.

We hold no illusion that our suggested route to revitalization will be easy. It is grounded, however, in the simple ironic wisdom that is already emergent in many mainstream congregations:

Churches whose primary concern is making people full of God are also churches whose pews will be full of people.

Indeed, that statement is so simple-sounding that it is easy to miss its point. After politely listening to a recent presentation of our proposal at a clergy conference, the pastor of a growing (at least a little) and socially involved (at least a little) church stood up and shared how pleased he was that we were affirming H. Richard Niebuhr's "love of God and love of neighbor."

"Precisely," we respond, "except that we want to punctuate what many mainstreamers seem to forget. Niebuhr, following the gospel, *put devotion to God first!*"

NOTES

PREFACE

1. Dean R. Hoge and David A. Roozen, eds., *Understanding Church Growth and Decline: 1950–1978* (New York: Pilgrim Press, 1979).
2. Bruce Greer, "Strategies for Evangelism and Growth in Three Denominations (1965–1990)," *Church and Denominational Growth*, ed. David A. Roozen and C. Kirk Hadaway (Nashville: Abingdon Press, 1993), pp. 97-102.
3. Milton J. Coalter, John M. Mulder, and Louis B. Weeks, "Introduction," *The Mainstream Protestant "Decline,"* ed. Milton J. Coalter, John M. Mulder, and Louis B. Weeks (Louisville, Ky.: Westminster/John Knox, 1990), p. 17.
4. David A. Roozen and C. Kirk Hadaway, eds., *Church and Denominational Growth* (Nashville: Abingdon Press, 1993).
5. Jackson Carroll and Wade Clark Roof, "Introduction," *Beyond Establishment: Protestant Identity in a Post-Protestant World*, ed. Jackson Carroll and Wade Clark Roof (Louisville, Ky.: Westminster/John Knox Press, 1993), p. 11.
6. James Davidson Hunter, *Culture Wars: The Struggle to Define America* (New York: Basic Books, 1991).
7. For a review and critique, see Max L. Stackhouse, *Apologia: Contextualization, Globalization, and Mission in Theological Education* (Grand Rapids: William B. Eerdmans Publishing Co., 1988).
8. Robert N. Bellah, Richard Madsen, William M. Sullivan, Ann Swidler, and Steven M. Tipton, *Habits of the Heart* (Berkeley: University of California Press, 1985).
9. R. Stephen Warner, "Work in Progress Toward a New Paradigm for the Sociological Study of Religion in the United States," *American Journal of Sociology*, vol. 98 (1993), pp. 1044-93.

CHAPTER ONE: Where We Are, and from Whence We Came

1. "The Year's Top Stories," *The Christian Century* (December 22-29, 1993), p. 1291.
2. Ibid.
3. The concept of "under-churched" Americans was suggested in a conversation with Penny Long Marler. It is similar to the concept of "marginal members"—persons who retain a religious identity and church membership, but rarely participate in church activities.

4. Terry Mattingly, Scripps Howard News Service press release.

5. "The Year's Top Stories," p. 1293.

6. Ibid., pp. 1292-3.

7. Ibid., pp. 1291-2.

8. Ibid., p. 1293.

9. The "cultural center" today is much harder to define, and may no longer exist.

10. See Kenneth Bedell, *Yearbook of American and Canadian Churches* (Nashville: Abingdon Press, 1993), and earlier volumes.

11. Ibid. Statistics are from various volumes of the *Yearbook of American and Canadian Churches* and are supplemented by denominational yearbooks and minutes. Statistics have been adjusted for mergers, splits, and definitional changes. In addition, membership plots for each denomination were statistically "smoothed" to eliminate problems with anomalous years of reporting (prior to aggregation or averaging).

12. Most retain a conversionist orientation to the larger culture, and power often flows from personal charisma, rather than from institutional position. This is particularly true in denominations that have large numbers of megachurches.

13. See Steven Tipton, *Getting Saved from the Sixties* (Berkeley: University of California Press, 1982).

14. Wade Clark Roof and William McKinney, Jr., *American Mainline Religion* (New Brunswick, N.J.: Rutgers University Press, 1987); C. Kirk Hadaway and Penny Long Marler, "All in the Family: Religious Mobility in America," *Review of Religious Research*, vol. 35 (1993), pp. 97-116.

15. Wade Clark Roof and Mary Johnson, "Baby Boomers and the Return to the Churches," *Church and Denominational Growth*, ed. David A. Roozen and C. Kirk Hadaway (Nashville: Abingdon Press, 1993), pp. 293-310.

16. Poll-based statistics on Roman Catholics suggest problems that are masked by official membership records. The proportion of Catholics claiming membership and regular attendance has fallen, whereas switching to other denominations has increased. See Michael Hout and Andrew M. Greeley, "The Center Doesn't Hold: Church Attendance in the United States, 1940–1984," *American Sociological Review*, vol. 52 (1987), pp. 325-45; Hadaway and Marler, "All in the Family."

17. Hart M. Nelsen and Conrad L. Kanagy, "Churched and Unchurched Black Americans," *Church and Denominational*

Growth, ed. David A. Roozen and C. Kirk Hadaway (Nashville: Abingdon Press, 1993), p. 312.

18. Penny Long Marler and C. Kirk Hadaway, "New Church Development and Denominational Growth (1950–1988): Symptom or Cause?" *Church and Denominational Growth*, ed. David A. Roozen and C. Kirk Hadaway (Nashville: Abingdon Press, 1993), pp. 47-86.
19. Nelsen and Kanagy, "Churched and Unchurched Black Americans."
20. Hart M. Nelsen and Anne K. Nelsen, *Black Church in the Sixties* (Lexington: University Press of Kentucky, 1975).
21. Nelsen and Kanagy, "Churched and Unchurched Black Americans."
22. See C. Eric Lincoln and Lawrence H. Mamiya, *The Black Church in the African American Experience* (Durham, N.C.: Duke University Press, 1990).
23. See James Davidson Hunter, *Culture Wars: The Struggle to Define America* (New York: Basic Books, 1991).
24. See Jackson W. Carroll and Penny Long Marler, "Culture Wars? Insights from Ethnographies of Two Protestant Seminaries," *Sociology of Religion* (forthcoming, 1994).

CHAPTER TWO: Making the Church Choice

1. These conclusions are based on data published in various issues of *Emerging Trends* and Gallup's "Religion in America" series (Princeton, N.J.: The Gallup Organization).
2. C. Kirk Hadaway, Penny Long Marler, and Mark Chaves, "What the Polls Don't Show: A Closer Look at U.S. Church Attendance," *American Sociological Review*, vol. 58 (1993), p. 741. Also see Michael Hout and Andrew M. Greeley, "The Center Doesn't Hold: Church Attendance in the United States, 1940–1984," *American Sociological Review*, vol. 52 (1987), pp. 325-45.
3. These data are from various issues of *Emerging Trends* and Gallup's "Religion in America" series.
4. Theodore Caplow, Howard M. Bahr, and Bruce Chadwick, *All Faithful People: Change and Continuity in Middletown's Religion* (Minneapolis: University of Minnesota Press, 1983), p. 280.
5. Andrew M. Greeley, *Religious Change in America* (Cambridge, Mass.: Harvard University Press, 1989), p. 128.
6. David A. Roozen, "Church Dropouts: Changing Patterns of Disengagement and Reentry," *Review of Religious Research*, vol. 21 (1980), pp. 427-50.

7. Wade Clark Roof, *A Generation of Seekers* (San Francisco: Harper-Collins, 1993). Interviews with marginal church members conducted by Penny Long Marler and C. Kirk Hadaway reveal that many persons say they would return to the church if they had children. However, a few inactive Protestants who presently have children in the home said they might return to church when their children are grown.

8. See David A. Roozen, William McKinney, and Wayne Thompson, "The 'Big Chill' Generation Warms to Worship: A Research Note," *Review of Religious Research*, vol. 31 (1990), pp. 314-22.

9. Data are from various issues of *Emerging Trends*.

10. Hadaway, Marler, and Chaves, "What the Polls Don't Show," p. 742.

11. Ibid., pp. 747, 749-51.

12. Quoted by Kenneth L. Woodward, "Dead End for the Mainline," *Newsweek* (August 9, 1993), p. 47.

13. Penny Long Marler and David A. Roozen, "From Church Tradition to Consumer Choice: The Gallup Surveys of the Unchurched American," *Church and Denominational Growth*, ed. David A. Roozen and C. Kirk Hadaway (Nashville: Abingdon Press, 1993), p. 270.

14. Anthony Giddens, *Modernity and Self-Identity: Self and Society in the Late Modern Age* (Stanford, Calif.: Stanford University Press, 1991), p. 5.

15. Marler and Roozen, "From Church Tradition to Consumer Choice," p. 277.

16. Harold Bloom, *The American Religion: The Emergence of the Post-Christian Nation* (New York: Simon & Schuster, 1992), pp. 49-57.

17. Rush Limbaugh, *The Way Things Ought to Be* (New York: Pocket Books, 1992), p. 267.

18. Marler and Roozen, "From Church Tradition to Consumer Choice," pp. 267-68.

19. C. Kirk Hadaway and Penny Long Marler, "All in the Family: Religious Mobility in America," *Review of Religious Research*, vol. 35 (1993), pp. 97-116.

20. See Ann Swidler, "Culture in Action: Symbols and Strategies," *American Sociological Review*, vol. 51 (1986), pp. 273-86.

CHAPTER THREE: The Congregation:
When Radical Change Is Required

1. David A. Roozen and Jackson W. Carroll, "Recent Trends in Church Membership and Participation," *Understanding Church*

Growth and Decline, ed. Dean R. Hoge and David A. Roozen (New York: Pilgrim Press, 1979), pp. 38-40.

2. See Kenneth W. Inskeep, "A Short History of Church Growth Research," *Church and Denominational Growth,* ed. David A. Roozen and C. Kirk Hadaway (Nashville: Abingdon Press, 1993), pp. 135-48.

3. C. Kirk Hadaway, *Church Growth Principles: Separating Fact from Fiction* (Nashville: Broadman Press, 1991).

4. Even when other factors are controlled, the age of a church is strongly related to church-membership change in Kirk Hadaway's work on evangelism and church growth among Southern Baptist churches, and in research on mainstream churches by Michael Donahue and Peter Benson. In addition, Penny Marler and Kirk Hadaway show that church age is strongly related to church growth in mainstream and evangelical denominations. See C. Kirk Hadaway, "Is Evangelistic Activity Related to Church Growth?" *Church and Denominational Growth,* ed. David A. Roozen and C. Kirk Hadaway, pp. 169-87; Michael J. Donahue and Peter L. Benson, "Belief Style, Congregational Climate, and Program Quality," *Church and Denominational Growth,* ed. Roozen and Hadaway, pp. 225-40; Penny Long Marler and C. Kirk Hadaway, "New Church Development and Denominational Growth (1950–1988): Symptom or Cause?" in *Research in the Social Scientific Study of Religion, Vol. 4,* ed. Monty L. Lynn and David O. Moberg (Greenwich, Conn.: JAI Press, 1992).

5. Ibid.

6. Daniel V. A. Olson, "Church Friendships: Boon or Barrier to Church Growth?" *Journal for the Scientific Study of Religion,* vol. 28 (1989), pp. 432-47.

7. Other types of movements exist, including those that seek to reform society by accomplishing more "liberal" goals.

8. Wayne L. Thompson, Jackson W. Carroll, and Dean R. Hoge, "Growth or Decline in Presbyterian Congregations," *Church and Denominational Growth,* ed. Roozen and Hadaway, pp. 188-207.

9. Marjorie H. Royle, "The Effect of a Church Growth Strategy on United Church of Christ Congregations," *Church and Denominational Growth,* ed. Roozen and Hadaway, pp. 155-68; C. Kirk Hadaway, "Do Church Growth Consultations Really Work?" *Church and Denominational Growth,* ed. Roozen and Hadaway, pp. 149-54.

10. Kenneth W. Inskeep, "A Short History of Church Growth Research."

11. Daniel V. A. Olson, "Congregational Growth and Decline in Indiana Among Five Mainline Denominations," *Church and Denominational Growth,* ed. Roozen and Hadaway, pp. 221-24.

12. C. Kirk Hadaway, "Conservatism and Social Strength in a Liberal Denomination," *Review of Religious Research,* vol. 21 (1980), pp. 321-37; C. Kirk Hadaway, "From Stability to Growth: A Study of Factors Related to the Statistical Revitalization of Southern Baptist Congregations," *Journal for the Scientific Study of Religion,* vol. 30 (1991), pp. 181-92.

13. Thompson, Carroll, and Hoge, "Growth or Decline in Presbyterian Congregations."

14. Dean M. Kelley, *Why Conservative Churches Are Growing,* Rev. Ed. (New York: Harper & Row, 1977).

15. Roger Finke and Rodney Stark, *The Churching of America, 1776–1990* (New Brunswick, N.J.: Rutgers University Press, 1992); Laurence R. Iannaccone, "Why Strict Churches Are Strong," *American Journal of Sociology,* vol. 99 (1994), pp. 1180-211.

16. Kennon L. Callahan, *Twelve Keys to an Effective Church* (San Francisco: Harper & Row, 1983).

17. See Norman Shawchuck and Gustave Rath, *Benchmarks of Quality in the Church* (Nashville: Abingdon Press, 1994).

CHAPTER FOUR: Mainstream Church Growth

1. Martin Marty, "Counterevidence," *The Christian Century* (October 27, 1993), p. 1071.

2. Peter L. Benson and Carolyn H. Eklin, *Effective Christian Education: A Summary Report on Faith, Loyalty, and Congregational Life* (Minneapolis: Search Institute, 1990), p. 51.

3. Leonard Sweet, "Can a Mainstream Change Its Course?" in *Liberal Protestantism,* ed. Robert S. Michaelson and Wade Clark Roof (New York: Pilgrim Press, 1986), pp. 237-38.

4. Stephen L. Carter, *The Culture of Disbelief* (New York: Basic Books, 1993).

5. According to Carl Dudley, we have made pluralism our dominant "ism." Carl Dudley, "Pluralism as an ism," *The Christian Century* (October 27, 1993), p. 1040.

6. Jackson W. Carroll, "Horizontal Religion," *The Christian Century* (October 13, 1993), p. 966.

7. This conclusion is based on interviews conducted by Penny Long Marler and C. Kirk Hadaway with agnostic and atheist marginal Protestants.

8. Sweet, "Can a Mainstream Change Its Course?"
9. Obviously, mainline Christians will carry on certain activities that are, in fact, evangelism. But they will resist calling them "evangelism."
10. Sweet, "Can a Mainstream Change Its Course?"
11. Shirley C. Guthrie, Jr., "The Nearness and Distance of God," *Transcendence and Mystery*, ed. Earl D. C. Brewer (New York: IDOC/North America, 1975), p. 37.
12. Ted Loder, "Prayers for the Battle," *Guerrillas of Grace* (San Diego: LuraMedia, 1984). Taken from the worship schedule of the Federated Church, United Church of Christ, Chagrin Falls, Ohio (Sunday, January 16, 1994).
13. Donald E. Miller, "Liberal Church Growth: A Case Study," unpublished paper presented at the 1989 meetings of the Society for the Scientific Study of Religion, p. 26.
14. Peter L. Berger, *The Heretical Imperative* (Garden City, N.Y.: Anchor Press, 1979), pp. 59-60 (emphasis added).
15. Sweet, "Can a Mainstream Change Its Course?" p. 239.
16. Personal communication on the electronic superhighway from Thomas Dipko to Kirk Hadaway (December 1993).
17. Questions like this were raised frequently by unchurched and underchurched Protestants interviewed by Penny Long Marler and C. Kirk Hadaway, as part of their Lilly-funded study of religious marginality. Many persons leave the church after traumatic personal crises, often involving the death of a loved one. All too frequently, no one from the person's church even tried to help them through what had happened.
18. Peter L. Berger, *The Heretical Imperative*, p. 139 (emphasis added).
19. Barbara Doherty spoke of this "Jinana," or "gut energy"—one who understands—in a lecture, "The Diversity of Spirituality in the Communities of Learners," at Valparasio University, October 9, 1993.

CHAPTER FIVE: The Denomination: How Institutions Help or Hurt

1. Roger Finke and Rodney Stark, *The Churching of America, 1776–1990* (New Brunswick, N.J.: Rutgers University Press, 1992).
2. See Ernst Troeltsch, *The Social Teachings of the Christian Churches*, trans. Olive Wyon (Louisville, Ky.: Westminster/John Knox, 1992).
3. Penny Long Marler and C. Kirk Hadaway, "New Church Development and Denominational Growth," *Church and Denominational*

Growth, ed. David A. Roozen and C. Kirk Hadaway (Nashville: Abingdon Press, 1993), p. 61.

4. James Davidson Hunter, "American Protestantism: Sorting Out the Present, Looking Toward the Future," *The Believable Futures of American Protestantism,* ed. J. Richard Neuhaus (Grand Rapids: William B. Eerdmans Publishing Co., 1988), p. 205.

5. Norval Glenn, "The Trend in 'No Religion' Responses to U.S. National Surveys, Late 1950s to Early 1980s," *Public Opinion Quarterly,* vol. 51 (1987).

6. Marler and Hadaway, "New Church Development and Denominational Growth," pp. 63-64.

7. Bruce A. Greer, "Strategies for Evangelism and Growth in Three Denominations (1965–1990)," *Church and Denominational Growth,* ed. David A. Roozen and C. Kirk Hadaway (Nashville: Abingdon Press, 1993).

8. Ibid., pp. 89, 91.

9. Ibid., p. 101.

10. John Ronsvalle and Sylvia Ronsvalle, *The State of Church Giving Through 1991* (Champaign, Ill.: The Empty Tomb, Inc., 1993). We do not believe that "straight-line projections" of this sort are valid. We reference this projection only to underscore the seriousness of the decline in giving to denominational causes.

11. Wade Clark Roof and William McKinney, *American Mainline Religion* (New Brunswick, N.J.: Rutgers University Press, 1988), pp. 158-62.

12. The vast majority are either growing or declining. See Marler and Hadaway, *New Church Development and Denominational Growth,* pp. 79, 85.

13. Ibid., pp. 82-83.

14. Laurence R. Iannaccone, "Why Strict Churches Are Strong," *American Journal of Sociology,* vol. 99 (1994), p. 9.

15. Dean M. Kelley, *Why Conservative Churches Are Growing,* Rev. Ed. (New York: Harper & Row, 1977); Finke and Stark, *The Churching of America, 1776–1990.*

16. Luther P. Gerlach and Virginia H. Hine, *People, Power, Change Movements of Social Transformation* (Indianapolis: The Bobbs-Merrill Co., 1970), p. 107.

17. Wayne L. Thompson, Jackson W. Carroll, and Dean R. Hoge, "Growth or Decline in Presbyterian Congregations," *Church and Denominational Growth,* ed. David A. Roozen and C. Kirk Hadaway (Nashville: Abingdon Press, 1993), p. 197.

CHAPTER SIX: Mainstream Movements

1. Leonard Kalkwarf, "Meeting at the Summit: President's Report to General Synod," *Church Herald*, vol. 41 (1984), p. 14. A passage regarding identity issues from this publication was quoted by Donald Luidens in "Between Myth and Hard Data: A Denomination Struggles with Identity," *Beyond Establishment: Protestant Identity in a Post-Protestant Age*, ed. Jackson Carroll and Wade Clark Roof (Louisville, Ky.: Westminster/John Knox Press, 1993), p. 257.

2. Jackson Carroll and Wade Clark Roof, "Introduction," *Beyond Establishment*, ed. Carroll and Roof, pp. 11-13. Also, see comment by Michael Kinnamon, "Disciples' Analysis . . . ," *The Christian Century* (October 27, 1993), p. 1069.

3. William McKinney, "So How Do We Turn Things Around?" unpublished address (Hartford, Conn., 1989), p. 3.

4. Martin Marty, *Righteous Empire: The Protestant Experience in America* (New York: Harper & Row, 1970), pp. 89-90.

5. Ibid., p. 154.

6. See James Davidson Hunter, *Culture Wars: The Struggle to Define America* (New York: Basic Books, 1991).

7. Leonard Sweet, "Can a Mainstream Change Its Course?" in *Liberal Protestantism*, ed. Robert S. Michaelson and Wade Clark Roof (New York: Pilgrim Press, 1986), pp. 243-44.

8. Ibid.

9. Leander Keck, *The Church Confident* (Nashville: Abingdon Press, 1993).

10. Penny Long Marler and C. Kirk Hadaway, "Toward a Typology of Protestant 'Marginal Members,'" *Review of Religious Research*, vol. 35 (1993), pp. 34-54.

11. Anthony F. C. Wallace, "Revitalization Movements: Some Theoretical Considerations for Their Comparative Study," *American Anthropologist*, vol. 58 (1956), pp. 264-81. Also, Anthony F. C. Wallace, *Religion: An Anthropological View* (New York: Random House, 1966).

12. Luther P. Gerlach and Virginia H. Hine, *People, Power, Change Movements of Social Transformation* (Indianapolis: The Bobbs-Merrill Co., 1970), pp. 33-78.